You Are Special

By
Alma Kern

Illustrated by Barbara Maas

Printed in the United States of America

Library of Congress
Cataloging in Publication Data
ISBN 0-9614955-0-2

Third Printing 1986

*Special thanks
to my husband
for his patient love,
his sound advice.*

*He helps me believe
that I am special.*

TABLE OF CONTENTS

A CHALLENGE

PART I

YOU ARE SPECIAL

You Are the Only You 10
You Are Somebody 11
You Are Made in God's Image 13
God Loves You 15
You Are Priceless 16
Jesus Paid the Price 18
You Are God's Child 20
Like Father, Like Child 21
Then Why? 23
For Your Own Good 25
Thy Will Be Done 27
Be Confident 29
Don't Put Yourself Down 31
You Count 33
You Are Talented 35
Just Average 37
God Is with You 39
God Is in You 41
Be Filled with Joy 43
God Understands 45

PART II

BE ALL YOU CAN BE

Believe You Can Change 49
Set Goals 50
Be Your Friend 51
Get Rid of Self-doubt 52
Love Yourself 53
Be Patient 54
You Can Be Beautiful 57
Let Jesus Be Lord 59
Study God's Word 60
Seek Him 63
Stop! Listen! 65
Meditate 67
Tap the Power 69
Have Faith 71
Give Thanks 73
Praise the Lord 75
Sing for Joy 76
Remember Him 77

5

Come for Supper 79
Open Your Life to God 81
When You Pray, Say 83
Mean What You Pray 85
Don't Worry 87
Replace Worry with Faith 89
Face Your Fears 91
Fears Need Not Stop You 93
You Can Take It 95
Keep On Going 99
Forgive Yourself 100
Take Heart 101
Admit Your Age 103
Are You Chasing Rainbows? 104
Thank God for Today 105
Use Time Wisely 106
Do It Now 107
Be All You Can Be 108

PART III

DO ALL YOU CAN DO

God Calls You 113
Be Willing to Serve 114
Let God Use You 115
Your Role Is Important 116
Love All God's Children 118
Talk About Jesus 121
Demonstrate God's Love 123
Receive Graciously 124
Say "Thank You" 125
Have a Word of Praise 127
Lend an Ear 129
Speak an Encouraging Word 130
Be Available 132
Forgive Others 133
Pray for a Forgiving Heart 134
Weep with Those Who Weep 135
Follow Jesus 137
Smile 138
Pray for Others 139
Do Something for Someone 140
God Will Reward You 141

A Challenge!

The lack of self-esteem is a universal problem. There is no magic formula that will enable you to develop self-confidence and the right kind of self-love. Nobody can give them to you. They must be nurtured within you day by day.

This book offers some positive thoughts to help assure you that *YOU ARE SPECIAL.*

God loves you just as you are, but He doesn't want you to remain what you are. He wants you to reach your full potential, to become all you can be.

You are not challenged to climb up to God to win His approval. God already stooped to your level when Jesus came down to this earth to die in your stead. Jesus makes you right with God. His Spirit is with you, willing to fill you. Become more aware of His presence and power. Let His thoughts seep into your mind and overflow into the rest of your life.

Accept yourself as you are, but never be satisfied with yourself as you are. Strive to be a becomer, always growing and changing. God is eager to reshape your life. But it also takes effort on your part.

You are on a God/human team to help other people. Our magnificent God can do tremendous things in you, with you and through you. He wants you to love the world as you love yourself. Since God makes your love of self the standard for loving others, it is extremely important to be convinced *YOU ARE SPECIAL!*

YOU ARE SPECIAL

You Are the Only You

There is nobody else like you — never was, never will be.

Does that make you laugh and say, "No wonder!
When God saw me, He threw away the pattern!"?

Or do you say, "Wow! I'm an original!
I'm a special me! Thank You, Lord!"?

Our amazing God likes variety.
No two trees are alike, not even two leaves.
It's no surprise that no two people are exactly the same.

Even your fingerprints are unique.
Over four billion people in the world have fingerprints
that are a positive identification.

You have emerged as God's special handiwork
with your own array of traits and skills.
You do not look, think, feel, speak, walk or
even write exactly like anybody else.

You are what you have been in all your yesterdays —
all you've seen, heard, read, thought, said and done.

Your background and experiences have come
together in a once-in-forever way.

Believe you are somebody special.
You can do something uniquely worthwhile.
You can make a difference!

You Are Somebody

Have you ever asked, "How come I am what I am?"

When we ask the question "WHY?", it is often a cry of bitterness. We should ask in a thankful spirit with a sense of wonderment: "Why was I born where I was? when I was? to the parents I had? Why was I given normal intelligence? In a world where so many cannot read or write, why did I have the opportunity to learn these skills? How come I've heard the Good News of God's love over and over again? Some people have never heard it once."

Some of us were born to parents who wanted us and rejoiced at our birth. They received us joyfully as precious gifts from God. They raised us as best they could.

Others seem to have been biological accidents, arriving unplanned, unexpected, unwelcomed and unloved.

No matter what the circumstances of your birth, you are not just a happenstance of nature. God made you! God uses the best intentions of people. He can also overrule the worst intentions to accomplish His purpose.

God once used a condemned child of a slave woman. By a remarkable twist of events the Lord not only preserved the life of that boy but also gave him the advantages of growing up in a palace. God used strange circumstances to raise up a leader for His ancient people. Yet, when God finally called Moses into special service, Moses asked, *"Who am I?"* (Exodus 3:11) He had self-doubts, felt unfit.

It didn't matter who Moses was or who he had been. What did matter was that God had called him. God wanted to make somebody special out of him.

When you ask, "How come I am what I am?" assure yourself: *"By the grace of God I am what I am."* (1 Corinthians 15:10)

> You are special. God made you.
> His undeserved love makes you somebody!

"So God created man in His own image,
in the image of God He created him;
male and female He created them."

Genesis 1:27

"Yet thou hast made him little less than God,
and dost crown him with glory and honor."

Psalm 8:5

Jesus "reflects the glory of God and bears the very stamp of
His nature. . . ."

Hebrews 1:3

"He is the image of the invisible God."

Colossians 1:15

". . . Be conformed to the image of His Son. . . ."

Romans 8:29

You Are Made in God's Image

The sign at the great ape house in the zoo reads:
"Do you know your roots?"

The same Creator who made all animals small and great
also made you. Naturally He reused some of the same
ideas — two eyes, a tongue, a heart.
But you are not the offspring of a chimp!
God made you in His own image.

Some people would have you believe you're just a
little higher than the animals. They say, "Do your
own thing. If it feels good, do it!"

The Bible says
you are made a little lower than the angels,
a little less than God!
What possibilities God sees in you!

You're more than a body and mind.
You have a spirit which will live forever.
This spirit enables you to communicate with your Maker.
You can know His will for your life. Your spirit was
made so that you can yearn for the Spirit of God.
You are incomplete without Him.

Respond to the Holy Spirit.
He will empower you and lift you up!
He wants to make you all you can be.

Sin has dimmed and blurred the image of God in you.
Only Jesus reflects perfectly the glory of God.
But praise the Lord, the more you imitate Christ,
the better your image.

"God is love . . . ."

1 John 4:16

*"This is love: not that we loved God,
but that He loved us and sent His Son
as an atoning sacrifice for our sins."*

1 John 4:10 NIV

God says, *"I have loved you
with an everlasting love . . . ."*

Jeremiah 31:3

*"You are precious in My eyes, and
honored, and I love you. . . ."*

Isaiah 43:4

God Loves You

God always loves you.

When you're glad,
        mad,
        sad,
        bad,
        God loves you.

God's love does not depend on how you feel.
When you feel great and the world is your apple,
        God loves you.
Though you feel miserable, discouraged, frightened,
        God loves you.
Even when you don't feel His presence,
bring Him shame and grief,
ignore or hate Him,
        God loves you.

When you think He doesn't love you,
and bitterly cry out, "Why?"
because you've lost the dearest and best,
        God loves you.

God doesn't love you because you are valuable.
You are valuable because God loves you.
He loves you with a love that gives, forgives.

Why?
        Because God is love.

You Are Priceless!

"You, therefore, must be perfect, as your heavenly Father is perfect." (Matthew 5:48) That's what Jesus says.

Like everybody else you fall short of God's standard of perfection. In fact, there is an appalling gap between what you are and what you are expected to be.

Fortunately, you do not have to qualify yourself to become worthy of God's love. Rather, His love qualifies you.

Your sins are deeply personal. So is God's solution. God became personally involved in your problem. He sent His Son to earth for your sake.

Jesus always did what was pleasing to His Father. Yet the Lord laid on Him the sins of every one. The only perfect, sinless Person in history was sacrificed. He paid the price for the wrongs you've done and the good you've left undone. God took the burden of guilt from your shoulders and placed it on His Son.

Jesus died a death He did not deserve that you might have a life you don't deserve. How far God was willing to go! He sacrificed His holy precious Son for you! God's pricetag on you is tremendously high. You are priceless!

What must you do to be saved?
  Believe in the Lord Jesus.
  Believe: Jesus lived the perfect life I fail to live.
            He died for me.
            Therefore, God accepts me just as I am.
            I'm justified —
            treated just-as-if-I'd never sinned.

"All we like sheep have gone astray;
we have turned every one to his own way;
and the Lord has laid on Him
the iniquity of us all."

Isaiah 53:6

"Since all have sinned and fall short
of the glory of God,
they are justified by His grace as a gift. . . ."

Romans 3:23,24

"We believe that we shall be saved
through the grace of the Lord Jesus. . . ."

Acts 15:11

"For by grace you have been saved through
faith; and this is not your own doing,
it is the gift of God — not because of
works, lest any man should boast. For
we are His workmanship, created in Christ
Jesus for good works, which God prepared
beforehand, that we should walk in them."

Ephesians 2:8–10

Jesus Paid the Price

Dear Lord,

You know: I love You.
I try to be good.
I try not to hurt anyone.
I help other people.
I live a good, clean life.
I've been baptized and confirmed.
I'm a good church member.
I do the best I can under the circumstances.
I do some wrong things, but
I try to make up for them.
I'm not perfect. Nobody is!

What do You expect?
Perfection?
But I can't be perfect!
When I look at the list above, they all start the same:
I . . . I . . . I . . . Too often I put me where You ought to be —
in the center of my life.

I need to remind myself:
my salvation does not rest on me.
It's impossible to save myself.

When I look at Jesus, I see what You are like.
You're great and good. You are loving.
But You are also just and You demand obedience.
When I look at Jesus' faultless life,
I see what You expect of me.
His goodness arouses in me
a sense of my guilt, my shortcomings.

He also awakens in me a spirit of thanksgiving and praise.
I thank and praise You, Jesus, for delivering me
from the penalty and power of my sin.
You did what was impossible for me to do for myself.

Father, You have redeemed me with the precious blood of
Jesus. In response to Your love
I'll live in a way that brings glory to Your name.
Help me in my struggle to love You more,
to help others and not hurt them, to live a good, clean
life, to be a good church member and always to do
the best I can.

Forgive my failures to live up to Your expectations.
I know I'm not perfect, Lord. But I rejoice that I'm forgiven.
                    Your grateful child.

You Are God's Child

Jesus tells you that you can approach the almighty
Maker of heaven and earth and call Him:
"Our Father, who art in heaven."

Matthew 6:9

Jesus made this relationship possible.
*"To all who received Him, who believed
in His name, He gave power to become
children of God."*

John 1:12

*"See what love the Father has given us,
that we should be called children of
God; and so we are."*

1 John 3:1

If you trust in Jesus as your personal Savior, you know you've
been adopted into the family of God. God chose you.
He raised you to this position of honor.
*"God sent forth His Son, born of woman,
born under the law, to redeem those who were
under the law, so that we might receive
adoption as sons. And because you are
sons, God has sent the Spirit of His Son
into our hearts, crying, 'Abba! Father!' "*

Galatians 4:4–6

God really loves you.
You are priceless in His sight.
He created you. He redeemed you.
You are His child.
God is the King of the universe.
That makes you a princess! a prince!

How much God expects of you! Wow!
He has exceedingly high expectations!

Like Father, Like Child

Dear Lord,

Thank You for sending Jesus into the world. Because of what He did I am Your forgiven child. I rejoice!

In Your Word I learn to call You "Abba, Father" — "Daddy, Father." What an honor! I feel comfortable coming to You with my problems and fears.

It's great to be loved! to be secure in Your protecting arms! to have my needs supplied!

But, Father, being Your child isn't always easy! You make some big demands of Your children.

It's hard to obey Your commands: Be servant of all. Pray for those who abuse you. Overcome evil with good. Yet Jesus teaches, *"Love your enemies . . . so that you may be sons of your Father who is in heaven."* (Matthew 5:44,45)

I fall short of so many of Your demands! Forgive me, Father. Forgive my weak desire to improve. Thank You for being so patient, kind and gentle with me.

Father, how merciful You are to me! Move me to show mercy to others. Please fill me with Your Spirit so that I may more and more strive for the perfection You desire. Help me be like Jesus, spending my life pleasing You and serving people.   Amen.

"For My thoughts are not your thoughts,
neither are your ways My ways,
says the Lord.
For as the heavens are higher than the earth,
so are My ways higher than your ways
and My thoughts than your thoughts."

Isaiah 55:8,9

"I consider that the sufferings of this
present time are not worth comparing with
the glory that is to be revealed to us."

Romans 8:18

"I am convinced that
neither death nor life,
neither angels nor demons,
neither the present, nor the future,
nor any powers,
neither height nor depth,
nor anything else in all creation,
will be able to separate us from the
love of God that is in Christ Jesus our Lord."

Romans 8:38,39 NIV

Then Why?

Did you ever wonder: since I'm God's child
and He loves me dearly,
then why did He let this happen to me?
to the one I love? Why does He allow suffering?
Why do bad things happen to good people?

God never promised us exemption from trouble.
Some pain, disappointment and grief
are a normal part of life.
As long as we live in this world,
we'll be subject to these robbers of happiness.
Only in the next life will our Lord wipe away
all tears from our eyes. This life is temporary.
So are its sorrows.

Often things happen to God's children that appear
to have no purpose. It's then we struggle
to understand God's ways.
We ask, "Why?" We want answers.
But God usually doesn't give an answer.
We simply don't know why.

We see only the here and now.
God sees the whole picture — here and everywhere,
now and forever — you and everybody else.
God sees all. Knows all.

What God knows is best differs vastly from
what we think is best.

God is not obligated to act only in ways we can understand.
God is not limited only to ideas that we can explain.

Since the Lord does not consider it needful that
we understand His reasons for doing what He does,
we live by faith. We receive comfort and strength knowing:
God is good — totally good.
He wants only good things for our lives.
*"We know that in everything God works for good
with those who love Him. . . ."* (Romans 8:28)

For Your Own Good

"Mommy, Mommy, why are you letting them do this to me?" the four-year-old screamed in terror and pain. A minor surgical procedure was being performed in the doctor's office. Her mother wept, too, as she tried to explain why it was necessary. The child could not see beyond the moment of misery. So the mother finally said simply, "Honey, it's for your own good."

A loving mother hurts to see her child suffer. Yet sometimes there must be seeming cruelty in love.

How my loving heavenly Father must also hurt when I am hurting from the blows of life!

Sometimes I suffer because of my own foolish mistakes. I can't blame God for that.

At other times I'm harmed because of somebody else's mistakes. I must not blame God for these things either. God is for me. It is Satan who would tear down my confidence in God's love.

I must remind myself: God makes no mistakes. Nothing surprises Him. He is never confused. He is always in control.

God allows me to have some unhappy experiences not to frustrate me but to discipline me. They push me into new directions and make me depend on Him for guidance. God works in mysterious ways His wonders to perform!

Dear Father in heaven,
Help me recognize Your loving hand
when You're leading me through dark valleys.
Forgive me for doubting Your wisdom and
thinking You are unfair.

I want to fit into Your loving plan.
But, Lord, I need Your strength.

I know things do not just happen by chance.
Since You permit some sad things to occur, I trust
that somehow You'll make them work together for my good.

Thy Will Be Done

Dear Lord,

It's very hard for me to pray, "Thy will be done," and really mean it.

Sometimes I mouth those words in passive submission only when it's evident that You are not going to do things my way.

What I mean at times like that is: I believed Your promise," Whatever you ask in prayer, believe that you receive it, and you will. "(Mark 11:24)

I told You what's wrong, what I need, what I want. I outlined what I'd like You to do. I coaxed, begged, tried to bargain. I believed You could work miracles. I waited for You to change things. But nothing happened. O.K., Lord, You win. Do it Your own way.

I guess at times I've tried to use You to do my will. Forgive me for acting like a frustrated little child who slams the door after receiving "no" for an answer.

Lord, help me remember that You are my loving, all-wise Father. Whatever You will for me is best for me. Your will is always good. You know what I don't know — things beyond my comprehension.

Father, increase my faith. Enable me to begin each day with the sincere prayer, "Lord, what is Your will for me today? What do You want me to do? to say? to be? Guide me. Use me to do Your will."

*"God is our refuge and strength,
a very present help in trouble."*

Psalm 46:1

*"I pray that out of His glorious riches
He may strengthen you with power
through His Spirit in your inner being."*

Ephesians 3:16 NIV

*"My grace is sufficient for you,
for My power is made perfect in weakness. . .
for when I am weak, then I am strong."*

2 Corinthians 12:9,10

*"I can do all things in Him
who strengthens me."*

Philippians 4:13

Be Confident

"Jesus said, 'Take away the stone.' " (John 11:39) Lazarus had been dead four days. To remove the door of the burial cave seemed futile, repulsive. But the people obeyed Jesus' command. And Lazarus came out!

Lord Jesus, I ought to be much more alive than I am! Knowing You love me should fill me with peace, joy, vibrant hope. You stand at the door of my heart and knock. If I open the door, You promise to come in. Lord, I'll make room for You. Live in me today. Help me rejoice in Your fellowship.

The man was paralyzed, his muscles shriveled and useless. Jesus said to him, "Rise, take up your bed and go home." (Luke 5:24) How could he possibly manage to get up and walk, much less carry his cot? Jesus' command gave him the power to do it.

O Lord, forgive my excuses: "I could never do that. It can't be done. It won't work." Strengthen me, Lord, to believe I can do what You tell me to do. You say, *"Deny yourself and take up your cross daily."* (Luke 9:23) Without You I can do nothing. Filled with Your power I can do all things.

"How can this be?" Mary asked. A virgin conceive and bear a son? Impossible! The angel's explanation was equally hard to understand, yet Mary believed. "I am the Lord's servant. May it be to me as you have said." (Luke 1:38) Mary expected a miracle. It happened!

Dear Lord, You tell me to do things that seem impossible. How can I love my enemies? do good to those who hate me? forgive those who hurt me? Increase my faith to believe that with You all things are possible. Help me expect miracles. I will live according to Your Word. May it happen to me as You have said.

When Jesus said, "Come," Peter got out of the boat and walked on the water. What an exciting, never-to-be-forgotten moment! But it didn't last. "When he saw the wind," he was frightened and started to sink. (Matthew 14:30) Peter thought of the risks involved. When he concentrated on his problems, his heart sank. So did he!

O Lord, sometimes I see the vision of all You want me to be and to do. I hear Your words of challenge and command. I believe You. I have noble intentions . . . but, Lord, I have problems — discouraging, perplexing problems. When I take my eyes off You, my troubles look insurmountable. Oh me of little faith! Lord, help my unbelief!

They had already washed their nets after toiling in vain all night. "Put out into the deep and let down your nets for a catch." (Luke 5:4) Indeed! The time and place seemed all wrong. The men were tired, ready to quit. Nevertheless they obeyed. And their nets were filled to the breaking point!

Lord, at times I toil and "catch" nothing; work hard, but get nowhere. Give me new hope and confidence. Fill me with Your Spirit's power. Guide me to say and do the loving, courageous thing. Help me bring glory to You today.

"Make them sit down in companies, about fifty each." (Luke 9:14) Invite 5000 people for lunch when all you have is five loaves and two fish? Impossible! Common sense told the Twelve to send the crowds away. Faith made them obey.

Father in heaven, common sense sometimes tells me to be overly concerned with circumstances beyond my control. You tell me not to be anxious about the future because You'll provide for all my needs. Help me believe Your promise. Give me the courage to invite others to sit at Your banquet table. Strengthen my faith in Your love, my confidence in Your power.

Don't Put Yourself Down

"I'm going to be in your town on business next week. Let's get together for a short visit to talk about old times and catch up on news."

What a sad letter of reply this woman received from her friend of many years! "You are coming to see a dull character. I never go far from home any more. In fact, I'm a recluse by the world's standards. I hope you are not disappointed in me. I'm so limited conversation-wise. I've tried to forget my past and live only today — no future."

This person didn't have anything good to say about herself. True, there had been some problems, but all was not bleak. She still had good health, a good job, a loving, supportive family and church. Why put herself down?

Conscientious people sometimes feel less capable than they really are. There is a wide gap between what they think they are and what they think others expect them to be. Life takes on a humdrum pattern of busyness as they strive to meet their never-never standards. As a result they always feel less than they want to be. They regard themselves as failures.

Little children have a silly poem which goes verse after verse like this: "When God passed out noses, I thought He said 'roses'; I asked for a big red one. When He passed out brains, I thought He said 'trains'; I was late and missed mine." As adults we continue to remind ourselves and others, "I haven't got it. I can't do it. I'm not this. I'm not that." We imply: when God made me, He made a big mistake.

Unfortunately many of us have grown up to believe it's noble to think lowly of ourselves. We assume that's humility.

Of course, Christians should not be proud of their intelligence, their looks, the things they've accumulated, their abilities or the chance they have to use them. These are undeserved gifts of God. This fact should keep us humble.

To be humble, however, does not mean we must feel inferior. To downgrade ourselves, to say we are worth little or nothing is actually an insult to the God who made us.

This statement of the apostle Paul is an example of genuine Christian humility:

> *"God has given me the wonderful privilege of telling everyone about this plan of His; and He has given me His power and special ability to do it well. Just think! Though I did nothing to deserve it, and though I am the most useless Christian there is, yet I was the one chosen for this special joy of telling the Gentiles the Glad News. . . ."*

Ephesians 3:7,8 TLB

Although Paul referred to himself as the "least of the saints," he recognized the gifts God had given him to do His work. In a way, it was all God's doing. But God did not do the work alone. God used Paul's intelligence, education and writing skills. He used Paul's willingness to risk life and limb to get His message across.

"To all who received Him, who believed in His name, He gave power to become children of God. . . ." (John 1:12) Each of us can say: "Jesus has come into my life. I believe in His name. God does not put me down. He builds me up. He gives me power. What kind of power? The power to become! To become what I ought to be — like my heavenly Father. I am God's child! I will become the best kind of me I can be — not for my glory but for His!"

You Count!

Perhaps they don't say it in words
but their attitudes and actions imply,
"You are a nobody. You don't count.
You mean nothing to us — absolutely nothing!"

People judge importance by what you have,
what you produce, what you can do for them.
They tend to forget:
You count!

Perhaps you are your own worst enemy.
A sense of guilt may weigh you down:
      wasted opportunities, wasted time,
      drained energy, drained mind,
      lost health, lost youth.
You tend to forget:
You count!

Regardless of what others think about you,
or what you think about yourself,
no matter how conditions change in your life,
your value to God never diminishes.

God looks at you in a different way.
He rewards you according to your faithfulness —
what you do with what you have
under the circumstances.

You can share His love with someone today
      by your smile,
      a touch of support,
      a word of encouragement,
      thankfulness for the smallest favor,

a patient, sympathetic ear,
a heart that doesn't wallow in self-pity
but expresses confidence in God's plan.

Every life that touches yours
is God's gift to you.
You are His gift to each of them.
If you're His gift to someone else,
you must be okay.
God doesn't give a useless gift!
He gives you as you are.
You count!

You Are Talented!

Name five things you do well.

Does it seem immodest to admit you do them well? Do you have difficulty naming five skills? How about two? Many have trouble discovering even one.

All people are not created equal. God in His love and wisdom has given us different kinds of talents and gifts. Some have many; others, few. We differ in intelligence, physical ability and spiritual blessings. Each has differing opportunities to develop and use his talents and gifts.

In His story about the talents Jesus emphasized this inequality. One servant received five talents; another, two; the next, only one — "each according to his ability." (Matthew 25:15)

The two-talent person gained only 40% as much as the five-talent man. Yet each heard exactly the same words of praise from the master, "Well done, good and faithful servant; you have been faithful. . . ."

God does not compare us with each other. He measures success by comparing what we've done with what we should have done. Our ability is the measure of our responsibility.

At the time our Lord told the parable, a talent was a very large sum of money. The man who had received just one talent was actually entrusted with a tremendous amount. But he buried his talent. His excuse was, "I was afraid." Instead the master accused him of being "wicked and lazy."

Most of us are one-talent people. Our abilities seem so ordinary we underestimate them or even fail to recognize them. All of us, however, have more ability than we dare or care to believe.

Some talents and gifts appear to be more important or more glamorous than others. But God doesn't look at things the way we do. Look at this list:

> "We have different gifts, according to the grace given us. If a man's gift is prophesying, let him use it in proportion to his faith. If it is serving, let him serve; if it is teaching, let him teach; if it is encouraging, let him encourage; if it is contributing to the needs of others, let him give generously; if it is leadership, let him govern diligently; if it is showing mercy, let him do it cheerfully." Romans 12:6–8 NIV

One day we all must stand before our Maker and give an account of the way we've used our life. He will judge us not by the number of talents and gifts He gave us, but by our faithfulness in developing and using them.

May each of us live in such a way that He can say, "Well done, good and faithful servant, you have been faithful over a little . . . enter into the joy of your master."

Just Average

His fingers flew over the keys.
The audience was electrified.
As I listened, I could not help but wonder:
How is it that some people are so much more gifted than others?
He plays difficult music with such ease
while I struggle to play hymns and simple songs.

When he was interviewed, the musician was referred to as a genius.
"Genius nothing!" he protested.
"I've practiced eight hours a day, seven days a week
for more than twenty years!"

Some people rise head and shoulders above the rest of us
because they believe they can.
They invest tremendous amounts of time and effort
to become all they can be.

Thomas Edison once said, "If we did all we are capable of
doing, we would astonish ourselves."
Jesus said, *"If you have faith . . . nothing will be impossible
to you."* (Matthew 17:20)

Lord, no wonder I'm just average in so many things I do.
It's not Your fault.
I've failed to make the most of my abilities and opportunities.
I've been content just to get by.

I don't want to be a champion.
But I do want to please You.

Help me recognize the gifts You've given me.
Increase my love for others.
Move me to do the best I can in every task —
whether it's in my home, church, community or place of business.

Only then do I love You, myself and others the way I should.
Lord, let my corner of the world be a better place
because I gave it my very best. Amen.

"Fear not, for I am with you,
be not dismayed, for I am your God;
I will strengthen you, I will help you,
I will uphold you with My victorious right hand."

Isaiah 41:10

"Be strong and of good courage;
be not frightened, neither be dismayed;
for the Lord your God is with you wherever you go."

Joshua 1:9

"Lo, I am with you always. . . ."

Matthew 28:20

"I fear no evil; for thou art with me. . . ."

Psalm 23:4

God Is with You

God is everywhere.
He fills the universe, the far-flung galaxies.
Yet God is more than a pervasive principle.
He is a personal being.

Down through the ages He promised to be with His
faithful, chosen people in a special way.
His presence brought benefits:
"Fear not, for I am with you."
"I will be with you and will bless you."

God's presence with His ancient people
did not eliminate all their problems.
But as long as they were obedient to Him,
He gave them guidance, strength and protection.

God has not promised to immunize you
from sorrow and trouble.
He does promise to be with you.
He will go with you wherever you go,
whatever you go through.
He will never fail nor forsake you.
He will give you courage and strength to do what must be done.
His everlasting arms will provide comfort and support.

God is with you.
He is your Father, your best Friend.
Open your heart to Him in utter honesty —
praising, rejoicing,
seeking, reaching,
crying, complaining.

Ask Him for guidance.
Rely on Him for protection.
Look for evidence of His love.

God is with you!
How blessed you are!
You've been blessed to be a blessing!

God Is in You

We are not meant to be alone.
We need other people.
That's why God placed us in families, in communities.

We also are not meant to be solo Christians.
That's why God placed us in the Church.
We strengthen each other when we worship together.
If one is weak or ailing — physically or spiritually —
the others can support, comfort and encourage.

Yet ultimately our relation to God is
a very personal affair.
God loves the whole world —
not just the vast multitude of people
but each person individually.

God's love is a One-to-one action.
It requires a one-to-One response.

Jesus died for you personally to wash away your sin.
Only you can believe that for you.
In fact, Jesus' sacrifice makes you right with God
only if you believe in Jesus as
your very own personal Savior.

What an intimate relation you then have with your Lord!
You can say, "Christ lives in me!"
Through Jesus you are in union with God.

What a high honor the Lord shows you:
"Do you not know that you are God's temple
and that God's Spirit dwells in you?" (1 Corinthians 3:16)

God wants to reach out with His love through you.
Others should be able to meet God in you.

Think of that!
God is at work in you!
You are special!

*"Let us come into His presence with thanksgiving;
let us make a joyful noise to Him with songs
of praise!"*

Psalm 95:2

*"Thy words became to me a joy and the
delight of my heart. . . ."*

Jeremiah 15:16

"In Thy presence there is fulness of joy. . . ."

Psalm 16:11

"The joy of the Lord is your strength."

Nehemiah 8:10

*"These things I have spoken to you,
that My joy may be in you,
and that your joy may be full."*

John 15:11

Be Filled with Joy

"I've got the joy, joy, joy, joy down in my heart . . .
down in my heart to stay."

At times the joy in our hearts bubbles over.
We rejoice and sing songs of praise to the Lord.
Our glad hearts proclaim His goodness.
All's well with our world!

Yet things are not always well with our world.
Troubles and problems may come at any time
overwhelming us with headaches and heartaches.
That's life!

But we can still have a joy down in our hearts.
Even hearts that are not happy can have joy.
Happiness depends on circumstances.
Joy is independent of what happens to us.
It is a deep-seated sense of well-being.

Trees weather storms successfully if their roots
go deep into the ground giving them nourishment and stability.
That's the way it is with us, too.
We need to grab hold of certain positive convictions.
They give us sustenance and strength to withstand
the storms of life.

Each of us must make truths like these personal:
God loves me.
He really cares what happens to me.
I am precious in His sight.
My life has a purpose.
God is in control.
All things are working together for my good.

God will give me strength to face any situation.
The struggles of this life will end.
I know I will live forever with my loving Lord.

We should say these thoughts over and over until we believe
them and let them become a part of our mindset.
As God's presence and truth become more real to us, so
will His promise:

>*"Your hearts will rejoice and no one will take
>your joy from you."* John 16:22

God Understands

Dear Lord,
You remind me that I am Your beloved child.
Knowing You love me makes me feel important.
I want to please You and others.
I try to play the role of servant,
but people are not always grateful.
Sometimes they take advantage of me.
In fact, at times I'm criticized for what I do.
     Do You understand how that hurts?

You say I'm somebody special.
That's a happy thought when I'm alone with You.
But it's quickly rubbed out by reality.
People make so many demands of me.
They push and pull me in all directions.
Do this! Do that! Go there! Come here!
At times I'd like to get away from it all.
     Do You understand what it's like to be bone weary?

You tell me to have faith.
But life is tough, Lord.
I see innocent people suffering
not only terrible physical pain but also mental anguish.
Some are crushed when those they love desert them.
Evil often seems to triumph.
The bad guys appear to win!
     Do You understand how hard it is to cope with injustice?

You say You're always with me.
Your promise comforts and strengthens me.
I should be able to face problems unafraid
and take on challenges with courage.
But discouragement, disappointment and pain
make You at times seem distant and indifferent.
I feel forsaken.
     Do You understand how awful it is to feel forsaken?

Forsaken? Lord Jesus, of course, You understand!
You really were forsaken — by God,
hanging on that dreadful cross
with the guilt of all mankind heaped upon Your head.
How far You had to go to
rescue all mankind from the terror of
God-forsakenness!
    You understand agony!

You, God's special, only begotten Child,
were willing to give up the full use of Your
majesty and power to take on the role of servant.
You went about doing good.
Yet You were criticized, rebuffed, rejected.
Friends disappointed, denied, betrayed You.
Though innocent, You were humiliated, tortured, executed.
    You understand injustice!

But evil did not triumph!
You are the Conqueror!
You rose the Victor over death!
What a great Lord and Savior You are!
Praise to Your glorious name!
I want to spend my life pleasing You.
I want to be like You, Jesus, a servant.

BE ALL YOU CAN BE

There is a broad gap
between what you are and
what you can be.

Remove the excuses and obstacles.
Deal with the hindrances and
blockages in your life.
Use the means God makes available
to change what you can.

Believe You Can Change

When we look in a mirror, we look for our faults. Only when we see what's wrong, can we make corrections. Once in a while there is not much we can do to improve ourselves. We slink away with a poor self-image: I look terrible. I'm sorry I looked.

We examine ourselves frequently so we can look better physically. We ought to do it for other reasons, too. Contrary to the maxim, what we don't know about ourselves often does hurt us. There is no substitute for honest self-appraisal.

Sometimes we know our faults, but we don't want to get rid of them. We feel comfortable with our flaws. We think less is expected of us if we admit: I'm very impatient. I have a bad temper. I'm afraid to do this or that.

Self-analysis is not enough. If we concentrate only on what's wrong with us, we deepen our sense of inferiority. Instead of being defeated or defensive, we should determine to overcome our faults.

We must want to change, believe we can change. God is ready to help us. He knows our potential. He promises to empower us.

Jesus used ordinary, faulty human beings to carry on His work. Although at times they demonstrated little faith, He didn't remind them they were worthless sinners. He told them, "Follow me." And they did. They learned from Him. They were transformed by His example. He changed them. They changed the world.

> God loves us — warts and all.
> But He doesn't want us to remain as we are.
> He wants us to be channels of His love.
> The Lord is willing to fill us with His Spirit.
> His power will lift us to a higher level.
> Only then can we be all we can be.

Set Goals

One of these days I ought to. . . . Someday I'd like to. . . . For weeks I've been wanting to. . . . If only I could. . . .

o Maybe it's something relatively simple:
  write certain letters, visit a shut-in, clean out the attic.
o Perhaps it's a project you've never attempted:
  read through the Bible, make a major trip, go back to school.
o Or maybe it's an undertaking that means sacrifice and effort:
  lose weight, change your job, volunteer your services.

How do you handle thoughts like these when they cross your mind? If you repeatedly push them aside without doing anything about them, they leave behind frustration and a lower opinion of yourself.

After a while the things you ought to do seem more and more formidable. You seem less and less able to deal with them.

Too often we don't improve because we don't plan to. We don't expect to be any better. We rise no higher than our expectation level.

Suggestions such as these will help:
1. Focus on the challenge you want to face first.
   After you succeed with this, you'll have more courage to take on the next.
2. Ask the Lord to enable you.
   Promise Him you'll do some definite things. Remember God doesn't do for you what you can do for yourself.
3. Set a specific, achievable goal.
   Write it down. Be realistic.
   A goal set too high makes you feel like a failure.
4. Set a timetable.
   Before this week is over . . . by the first of the month . . .
5. Assume you'll be able to do what has to be done.
   Picture yourself as an improved person.
6. Seek help from others.
   Tell somebody else your goal. That commits you.
   Join a group of people facing a similar challenge: an exercise class, weight loss group, Alcoholics Anonymous.
7. Start right away.

Be Your Friend

When you talk to yourself,
don't always pick on yourself.
Have an encouraging word.
Learn to say:
      "God loves you. So do I.
      He forgives you. So do I.
      Sometimes you disappoint and disgust me.
      You can improve.
      I'm going to do something about it!"

What you are now
has been shaped by your responses
to everything that has ever happened to you.

You will be what you are becoming.
Today you are determining
what you will be for the rest of your life.

You cannot control all that will happen to you.
You can determine how you will react to what happens.
When problems come — and come they will —
decide that with God's help
you will face them as challenges.
As you turn to your heavenly Father for strength,
each experience will make you a stronger person.

You know your limitations,
but God has given you also some good qualities.
Recognize them. Use them.

Start now to become the person you can be.
This is your life.
Make the most of it!

Get Rid of Self-doubt

Dear Lord,
just because some things went wrong,
I've had problems with self-doubt.

Sometimes I look at myself and wonder:
Much of my life is already gone.
What have I accomplished?

Help me get rid of dismal thoughts
and stop thinking of myself as a
f
  a
    i
     l
      u
       r
        e.

Thank You, Lord, for accepting me
at any level of faith or doubt.
The sacrifice of Jesus assures me of Your forgiving love.
Thank You for Your promise to be with me —
to fill me with Your Holy Spirit.

I believe Your promises.
To know You are here,
to know You love me
makes me feel better about myself.

I believe You will guide me
to make the right decisions
and give me power to do what must be done.

My faith is only the size of a mustard seed.
But I cling to Your promise:
nothing will be impossible.
Lord, I believe this. Help my unbelief.

Love Yourself!

There are no doubt some things you don't like about yourself. There are things about you God doesn't like either. He hates the sin in you. But He loves you anyway. The cross is positive proof of that. God desires your highest good. Dare to love yourself in the same way.

True self-love is not conceit. It is not feeling you are better than others. Healthy self-love recognizes all you are and have as gifts from God — totally undeserved.

Here are ways to improve your opinion of yourself:
1. Don't compare yourself with others.
   This might make you either sad or mad.
2. Never put yourself down.
   Don't concentrate only on what's wrong with you.
3. Don't let failure discourage you.
   Pick yourself up, dust yourself off and try again.
4. Learn from your mistakes.
   Don't be crippled by them.
5. Strive to improve yourself as much as you can.
   Pray for wisdom to discern between what can be changed and what cannot.
6. Ask for God's help to become all you can be.
   Believe His power will enable you.

A higher opinion of self leads to greater self-love. Only as you love yourself are you able to love your neighbor. Loving your neighbor will improve your opinion of yourself.

Be Patient

"Please be patient.
God isn't finished with me yet."
This is how most of us feel.
We long to be understood,
accepted for what we are,
tolerated in spite of our imperfections.

Impatience makes us short-tempered.
It causes us to do unkind things:
blow the horn if the car in front of us doesn't move quickly,
tell off a person who is late for an appointment,
criticize a spouse who forgets what he's been asked to do,
snap at a child who spills something.
Impatience makes it seem all-important
to be in the faster-moving line.
It makes us give up on a person who is slow to understand.

Impatience is egotistical.
It says, "I'm number one. I want to be in control.
My will should be done; my time schedule must be met.
I set the rules; everybody has to comply with my standards."
If people don't, we fuss, fume, rant, roar.
What a hindrance impatience is to our Christian witness!

God tells us, "Love is patient and kind."
Patience is the first element in love!
An impatient person is not kind, is often rude,
insists on his own way, is irritable.
In other words, without patience we do not love.
Without love we cannot live a God-pleasing life.

Patience is the nature of God.
He is not indulgent or permissive.
Eventually He punishes the unrepentant.
But He is slow to anger.
At all times God is love.
How thankful we can be that God is patient with us!

Our response should be to imitate His patient love.
To do that we need help.
We need His Spirit, His power.
When the Spirit controls us,
He produces in us love . . . patience.

Patience doesn't come instantly.
God permits annoying people and
vexing situations to appear.
That's His patience-training program for us.

When we are provoked and ready to blow our top,
most of us must do more than count to ten.
We need also to pray,
"Help! Lord, give me patience!"

"Charm is deceitful, and beauty is vain, but a woman who fears the Lord is to be praised."

Proverbs 31:30

"Let not yours be the outward adorning with braiding of hair, decoration of gold, and wearing of fine clothing, but let it be the hidden person of the heart with the imperishable jewel of a gentle and quiet spirit, which in God's sight is very precious."

1 Peter 3:3, 4

"The fruit of the Spirit is love, joy, peace, patience, kindness, goodness, faithfulness, gentleness, self-control. . . ."

Galatians 5:22

You Can Be Beautiful

The author of a book on how to be beautiful admits that beauty is not only her vocation but also her obsession. Besides cosmetics, diet and exercise tips, she recommends a great variety of treatments and surgery.

She herself has had her nose bobbed, eyelids undrooped with plastic surgery, laugh lines ironed out with silicone, skin smoothed with liver injections, hands chemically peeled, and her youth restored with cell therapy. She's gone through all this to improve the image in her mirror and the way she looks to others.

Most of us cannot afford or would not bother to have this kind of beauty treatment. So we must make the most of what we've got.

Our body is the temple of God's Holy Spirit. We ought to make it as pleasant to look at as possible. It is our duty to keep ourselves neat, clean, attractively groomed and dressed. We should eat the proper foods, get enough rest and exercise, and follow other sensible health rules.

Important as our body is, it's only our temporary dwelling. Its beauty fades rather quickly. Our inner nature — the real person in each of us — will someday move out and live forever in a different dimension.

For this reason the condition of our spiritual nature should be our primary concern. To be truly beautiful, we need to be like Jesus.

We should ask God to conform us to the image of His Son, to fill us with the fruit of His Spirit. This may require special treatments by God and perhaps some drastic surgery. It will also take daily effort on our part. But it will be worth it!

When love, joy, peace, patience, kindness, goodness, faithfulness, gentleness, self-control are evident in our lives, we will be beautiful — not just to look at but also to live with.

"Behold I stand at the door and knock;
if any one hears My voice and opens the door,
I will come in to him,
and eat with him, and he with Me."

Revelation 3:20

Jesus says,
"Why do you call Me 'Lord, Lord,'
and not do what I tell you?"

Luke 6:46

"If a man loves Me, he will keep My word,
and My Father will love him,
and We will come to him
and make Our home with him."

John 14:23

Let Jesus Be Lord

Before a guest arrives there are a few things most of us would like to straighten or clean.

If the guest stays only a short time, we can restrict her to rooms which are most presentable. But if her visit is a long one, this is harder to do. The guest makes herself at home and gradually gets to see us as we really are.

Some homes have the reminder "Christ is a guest at every meal, the unseen listener to every conversation." Jesus also sees the television programs we watch, the books and magazines we read. He observes the way we use our time, the things we do and say and think. He knows what our income is and how we spend our money.

Jesus not only watches us, He also wants to communicate with us. The Bible tells us: pray constantly. We are to talk with our Lord frequently and listen to what He tells us through His Word. God may also teach us through circumstances.

Sometimes we treat the Lord as an unwelcome guest. We feel uncomfortable knowing He's always around observing everything. At times we ignore Him and wish He'd do the same to us. When a problem arises, we like Him close by. Otherwise we'd like to confine Him to certain areas of our life and fit Him into our time schedule.

We would be insulted if a guest were to tell us to change our life-style, budget and timetable. That's what Jesus does. He's not satisfied to be merely an unseen guest. He wants to be manager. He wants to be in control. That means drastic adjustments on our part. It's not easy to say, "Jesus, I trust You as Savior. I trust You also as Lord of my life. Rule over me."

Only if we really mean that, will we become all we can be.

Study God's Word

The joy of discovery!

That can be our experience in daily personal Bible study. As we read and pray our way through its pages, our goal should not be to store up information. We are to seek to develop a deeper personal relation with the Author!

The following will help you get more out of Bible study:

Make an appointment with God.
> Keep it as faithfully as you would with a doctor — whether you feel like it or not.
> When you miss an appointment, apologize.
> Don't give up!

If possible, have a regular time and a certain place,
> when you can be at your best and receive the most,
> where you're least likely to be interrupted.

Begin your study with prayer.
> Ask: Lord, help me learn what You want me to learn,
>   do what You want me to do.
> Expect Him to answer!

Dig in! Think it out!
> Don't be discouraged by difficult parts.
> You're dealing with the mind of God.
> Don't be surprised if you don't understand all He says.
> Not everything will be of equal importance or interest to you.

Have a plan.
> Read one book. Start perhaps with Mark or John.
> Reread the same book. You'll always learn something new.
> Try reading the whole book at one sitting for a new view.
> Some days you'll want to read several chapters.
> Other times you may read only a few paragraphs.

Use a translation that's easy to read.
Comparing two translations often makes clear the meaning of a puzzling passage.

Keep one favorite copy of the Bible.
Write notes in it as you read.
Underline or highlight important verses.
Use the fly leaf to record verses you want to remember.

+   +   +   +

Expect to be blessed!
Desire to be a blessing!

"Seek the Lord and His strength,
seek His presence continually!"

1 Chronicles 16:11

"Seek the Lord while He may be found,
call upon Him while He is near. . . ."

Isaiah 55:6

"You will seek Me and find Me;
when you seek Me with all your heart,
I will be found by you, says the Lord."

Jeremiah 29:13, 14

Seek Him

Voices, sounds, noises!
How they drown out the "still, small voice"!
Even when we are alone, it's hard
to occupy our mind with thoughts of God.
Television, radio and newspaper take over
our thinking process.

Preoccupation with chores and cares
separates us from our heavenly Friend.
God then seems unreal and far away.
We almost forget about Him.

God seems no more real to us than we want Him to be.
"The Lord is near to all who call upon Him." Psalm 145:18

To become all we can be
we need to think deeply about our Lord.
We find Him in His Word, His will for our lives.

We must not wait until we find the time
to be alone with Him.
We must take the time.

This requires a strong desire to know God better.
To be molded by God, to become like Him
we must consciously seek Him.

If we seek Him, we find Him.

Stop! Listen!

I need a quiet place,
a quiet time
to be alone with God.

I have to stop,
to get in touch
with what I think and feel and believe,
to realign my thoughts,
to get it all together.

I have to be still
to experience the stillness
of God's presence,
to hear what He is saying,
to reflect upon His love.

I must open the doors of my mind
to let His bigness in.
He cares about me.
He believes I'm special.
He put me here for a purpose.

I am somebody!
I can do something special
for somebody else!

Verses for Meditation

"The Lord is my shepherd, I shall not want."

Psalm 23:1

*"God is our refuge and strength,
a very present help in trouble."*

Psalm 46:1

*"Fear not, for I am with you, be not dismayed,
for I am your God; I will strengthen you,
I will help you, I will uphold you with My
victorious right hand."*

Isaiah 41:10

"Do not be anxious about tomorrow. . . ."

Matthew 6:34

*"Peace I leave with you; My peace I give to you;
not as the world gives do I give to you.
Let not your hearts be troubled, neither let them be afraid."*

John 14:27

*"We know that in everything God works for good with
those who love Him,
who are called according to His purpose."*

Romans 8:28

"I can do all things in Him who strengthens me."

Philippians 4:13

Meditate

Anxiety and tension are among the leading complaints doctors hear. Often the prescription is a tranquilizer. God's people have known for thousands of years: meditation is medication!

In Christian meditation we ponder a Bible truth, mull it over in our mind.

The psalmist says one is blessed who meditates day and night. Try it at night when you cannot sleep and during the day when you are under stress.

These ideas will help you:

* Ask the Holy Spirit to guide you.
    Remind yourself He surrounds you.
* Block out disturbing thoughts.
    If past failures come to mind, confess them and enjoy
    God's forgiving love.
* Be honest to God.
    Don't be afraid to talk over your doubts.
    He's already aware of them.
    It will help you to admit them.
* Fill your mind with thoughts of God's love.
    Jesus is your friend.
    He gave His life for you.
    How good God is!
* Concentrate on a Bible verse or truth of Scripture.
    Repeat this verse or thought over and over.
    Ask: What is God telling me?
          What does He want me to do?
    Let God's words seep deep into your consciousness.

*   *   *   *

Meditation will refresh, renew and
strengthen you for crises and opportunities.

*"You shall receive power when the Holy Spirit
has come upon you. . . ."*

Acts 1:8

*"Be strong in the Lord and in the strength
of His might."*

Ephesians 6:10

*"My grace is sufficient for you,
for My power is made perfect in weakness."*

2 Corinthians 12:9

*"But they who wait for the Lord
shall renew their strength,
they shall mount up with wings like eagles,
they shall run and not be weary,
they shall walk and not faint."*

Isaiah 40:31

Tap the Power

A tremendous amount of electricity is made available by the power and light company. With it we can light up our homes and operate dozens of appliances. They turn, spin, whirl, heat, cool, bring pictures and music, record sound and information. What a difference power makes in our lives!

If we don't turn the switches, the house stays dark and appliances are useless. Power does no good unless we use it. It is not forced upon us.

The almighty Creator fills the whole universe with His power. He offers it to us. But He doesn't make us use it. We have to want it, ask for it, be willing to use it.

What a difference God's power can make in our life! It can bring out the great potential in each of us.

When we depend upon God's power to support and enable us, we are equal to anything we must face. We know we can do whatever we ought to do.

The human mind is a powerful instrument. It can send out forces that activate our body — even a weary, aching, faltering body. Let us fill our minds with reinforcing thoughts:

> God will supply me with the power I need
> when I need it.
> I can cope with anything this life may bring.
> I will apply God's power to whatever problem is mine.

*   *   *   *

> God's power is immense and wonderful!
> It lights up my life!

"Believe in the Lord Jesus, and you will be saved. . . ."

Acts 16:31

"We walk by faith, not by sight."

2 Corinthians 5:7

"Then Jesus answered her, 'O woman, great is your faith! Be it done for you as you desire.' "

Matthew 15:28

"Whatever you ask in prayer, you will receive, if you have faith."

Matthew 21:22

"All things are possible to him who believes."

Mark 9:23

Have Faith

Faith is believing . . .
>you are saved because you trust in Jesus.
>He died that you can live forever.
>eternal life is yours right now.

Faith is knowing . . .
>God loves you.
>He is always with you.
>He keeps His promises.

Faith is remembering . . .
>God is in control.
>He has a pattern for your life.
>He turns evil into good for those who love Him.

Faith is expecting God to . . .
>provide for all your needs.
>help you face trials and troubles.
>enable you to cope and to conquer.

Faith is being sure . . .
>God answers all your prayers.
>He gives you only what is best for you.
>He will never fail you or forsake you.

Faith is realizing . . .
>God can change you.
>He is able to work wonders in you.
>He wants to work through you.

"Give thanks in all circumstances;
for this is the will of God in
Christ Jesus for you."

1 Thessalonians 5:18

"Enter His gates with thanksgiving,
and His courts with praise!
Give thanks to Him, bless His name!
For the Lord is good;
His steadfast love endures for ever,
and His faithfulness to all generations."

Psalm 100:4, 5

Give Thanks To God

We need to develop an attitude of gratitude.
Otherwise we take our blessings for granted —
assuming we deserve all the good things of life.

If we learn to say "thank You" when things go well,
we are more apt to say "thank You"
even when things go wrong.

Troubles tend to make us lose sight of everything good
that went before, all that is still good in our lives.

Sometimes things seem so hopeless we even doubt God's love.
We turn away from Him in disappointment.
We concentrate on what's sad or bad.
We become bitter. We grumble and complain.
We get bogged down in despair.

A thankful heart moves us to dwell
        not only on what is wrong, but on what is right,
        not only on what we don't have, but on what we do have,
        not only on what is lost, but on what is left.
There is some good in every misery.
A discerning spirit finds reasons to be grateful.

A thankful heart can see God's goodness
in the most painful situation.
In spite of our troubles,
in the midst of our difficulties
God's love is the foundation fact of our life.
His presence gives comfort and confidence.
"We know that all that happens to us is working
for our good if we love God and are fitting into
His plans."   (Romans 8:28 LB)

Even when our face is streaked with tears,
a thankful heart prompts us to praise the Lord.

"Great is the Lord,
and greatly to be praised. . . ."

Psalm 145:3

"Praise the Lord!
Praise the Lord, O my soul!
I will praise the Lord as long as I live. . . ."

Psalm 146:1, 2

"Praise the Lord!
O give thanks to the Lord, for He is good;
for His steadfast love endures for ever!"

Psalm 106:1

"From the rising of the sun to its setting
the name of the Lord is to be praised!"

Psalm 113:3

"Let everything that breathes praise the Lord!
Praise the Lord!"

Psalm 150:6

Praise the Lord

God is our Maker, our Savior, our Provider.
All we are, have and hope to be are from Him.
How normal it ought to be for us to praise Him!

Day and night the heavenly creatures never stop saying,
"Holy, holy, holy, is the Lord God Almighty." (Revelation 4:8)
They cast their crowns before the throne singing His praises.

God wants our praise, too!
We're linked with heavenly beings by our praise!
What an awesome thought!

"O magnify the Lord with me," says the psalmist. (Psalm 34:3)
To magnify means to make an object appear larger than it is.
God is infinite! We can't make Him appear any greater!
We need to bring His boundless greatness into proper
focus for our own sake.

When we tell God how great and good He is,
we remind ourselves of the limitless power,
wisdom and love of the almighty Lord we worship.

We also praise God by telling others how good He is,
how He gives us strength and comfort and peace.
We praise the Lord by relating how He has answered
specific prayers.
We praise the Lord when we testify to what Jesus has
done and is doing for us. He is praised when we urge
others to accept His love.

God is not greater because we praise Him, but we are
greater when we praise Him. Praise gives rise to joy,
and joy in the Lord produces undergirding strength.

Sing for Joy

Heavenly Father,
You are great and good!
You pour Your love into my heart so that it overflows.
I will sing a song of praise today.

Down through the ages Your people have
praised You with singing —
with trumpets, harps, clanging cymbals.
You must enjoy the enthusiastic response of
thankful, joyful, love-full hearts.

Father, forgive me for sometimes being dull
of heart and mind when I worship You.
Pardon me for often singing Your praises
with so little zeal and zip.

Help me remember it's not the melody that counts
or the quality of the voice.
These please the ears of people.
You listen to the heart.

You despise worship that is insincere.
Fill my heart with clean thoughts and right desires.

Then I will walk in Your way
and sing for joy as I go.

Remember Him

"Take, eat, this is My body."
How those words must have baffled Jesus' disciples!
"Drink . . . this is My blood."
What a repulsive thought!
Blood! The element of life — and of sacrifice!

How could this be?
Jesus was right there at the table with them.
They had just finished the Passover meal.
A lamb had been slain earlier that day.
Its blood was poured out for them.
They had recalled God's great act of deliverance:
His rescue of His people from slavery.
The night before, an angel of death had stalked
the land of Egypt striking down the firstborn.
He spared the homes of God's people because the blood of
a lamb had been painted over their doorways.

The disciples didn't know this was the night before
God's new and greater act of deliverance.
Jesus, their companion and teacher, was soon to be the Lamb.
His holy, precious blood would be poured out for many.

How could bread and wine be flesh and blood?
Jesus' friends could not understand this great mystery.
They ate and drank in faith —
believing their beloved Friend was giving something
to uplift and strengthen them.
In this simple meal they would remember Him.
Through it they would proclaim His death until His return.

Bread, wine, body, blood.
The elements are still the same.
The mystery is just as great.
We eat and drink in faith.
The Lord's Supper draws us nearer to Him.
It assures us of our forgiveness and gives us new strength.

Come for Supper

"Take, eat, this is My body . . .
Take, drink . . . this is My blood . . ."
The pastor's voice recites the words.
I am kneeling before the altar.
But I am transported across time and space
to a supper table in an upper room.

Jesus is speaking to me personally.
I taste the bread and sip the wine.
It's hard to swallow them — for I remember His death.
This is His body offered for me.
His blood was shed for my sins —
all the bad things I've done, the good I've failed to do.
How much He loves me!

Here at His table
I feel a close bond with Peter, James and John —
with all believers who have faithfully
proclaimed the Lord's death for nearly two thousand years
so I could kneel here beneath the cross today.

"Depart in peace."
It's time to leave this place — the upper room — the altar rail.
I must return to mundane things of everyday life.

As bread and wine are now a part of me,
I'm reassured that Jesus is in me.
He goes with me into the nitty-gritty world.
His love will then motivate me.
His thoughts are to be my thoughts;
His will, mine.
He gave His life for me. I give my life to Him.

Holy Communion has made the Lord's loving presence more real
      to me.
I've received pardon for yesterday and strength for today.
I go now to serve with love! joy! peace!

"Before they call I will answer,
while they are yet speaking I will hear."

Isaiah 65:24

"Let us then with confidence
draw near to the throne of grace,
that we may receive mercy
and find grace to help in time of need."

Hebrews 4:16

"Ask, and it will be given you;
seek, and you will find;
knock, and it will be opened to you."

Matthew 7:7

"Ask, and you will receive,
that your joy may be full."

John 16:24

"Pray constantly."

1 Thessalonians 5:17

Open Your Life to God

Why pray?
God knows everything.

True! ". . . your Father knows what you need
before you ask Him." (Matthew 6:8)
Prayer is not informing God of what's going on.
The Almighty is not waiting for us to give Him directions.

Proper prayer does not try to manipulate God.
It is not an attempt to bring Him under our control.
It is not demanding God's help but
making ourselves more receptive to His power.
The real essence of prayer is the opening
of our lives to the influence of the living Lord.
It is lining up our will with His.
It's discovering what we really need.

Prayer is drawing nearer to God,
seeking to commune with the Eternal One.
For this reason prayer goes far beyond petition.
It is a blend also of thanksgiving, praise,
meditation and confession.

The more we pray, the closer we feel to God.
The closer we draw to Him, the more we are inclined to pray.
Faith gives us the confidence to pray.
Prayer exercises faith.
The stronger our faith in the Lord,
the more we rely on His goodness and greatness.

God's answers to prayer are not the only benefits.
Even in asking, a need is filled and we arise
strengthened and repaired.
The seeking, the asking, the knocking
are part of the blessing.
They remind us of our dependence on God
and make His presence more real.

Prayer can be a frantic outburst of supplication.
It is also calm, candid conversation.

On occasion God's answers to prayer are so dramatic
we call them miracles.
But a constant, quiet miracle takes place
in our hearts as we discover that
in answer to prayer, God supplies a steady flow of power
for ordinary daily living.
In opening ourselves to God's power,
we not only survive, we thrive!

When You Pray, Say . . .

OUR FATHER, WHO ART IN HEAVEN.
>Jesus tells me the almighty God,
>Creator of heaven and earth, is my Father.
>I rejoice in this intimate relationship.
>He is with me right now.
>He knows what I do, say and think!
>I pray as a loving child — confident that He hears.

HALLOWED BE THY NAME.
>God is holy.
>His name is holy.
>Whether or not I pray does not diminish God.
>Multitudes of heavenly beings worship the Lord.
>He permits me to join them in praising His name!
>What a lofty privilege that is!
>My tongue which sings His praises
>ought never to speak His name carelessly.
>All that I say and do should bring glory to His name
>and bring others closer to Him.

THY KINGDOM COME. THY WILL BE DONE . . .
>I look forward to heaven,
>where Jesus will rule in all His splendor.
>But I'm already in His kingdom!
>Jesus is Lord of my life.
>His will should be my command.
>Ah, there is a rift between
>what I am and what I ought to be.
>Often what Jesus expects of me is
>contrary to what I'd rather be doing.
>How my life needs to be conformed, reformed, transformed!

GIVE US THIS DAY . . .
>Material things occupy most of my waking thoughts —
>getting them, using them, maintaining them.
>All I have are gifts from my heavenly Father.

He knows my needs and will supply them.
This simple request reminds me to live one day at a time.
God is in control today, tomorrow and always.
He provides for the birds and flowers!
How much more He cares for me, His beloved child.
Faith replaces anxiety with thanksgiving.
Gratitude moves me to share His blessings.

FORGIVE US OUR TRESPASSES . . .

Our heavenly Father forgives and forgives and forgives.
Do some sins still haunt me?
Have I confessed them to God?
Do I want to give them up?
Do I believe Jesus' suffering paid for my sins?
If my answers are "yes," I can be positive that
God forgives and forgets.
I also want to have a forgiving heart.
I must forgive those who hurt and offend me.
For "If you do not forgive men their trespasses,
neither will your Father forgive your trespasses." (Matthew 6:15)

LEAD US NOT INTO TEMPTATION.

Satan will tempt me to sin today.
If I sin, it is my own fault.
The devil cannot make me do it.
I must be alert and resist temptation.
Satan is very powerful and also very clever.
Alone I'm no match for him. I need God's help.

THINE IS THE KINGDOM . . . POWER . . . GLORY.

I praise the Lord!
He is great and He is good!
In spite of what I see in the world around me,
I know God is in control.
To Him be all the glory now and forever.
Hallelujah! Praise the Lord!

AMEN.

This is certainly true!
God hears my prayer.

Mean What You Pray

Heavenly Father,
help me to pray.
Keep me aware of Your presence,
Your power, wisdom and love.

Forgive me for times when I
have just mouthed words,
empty phrases that slip across my lips.

Forgive me for sometimes praying half-heartedly,
not certain You were listening,
not sure You would answer.

Forgive my pride that keeps me
from seeing myself as You see me.

Forgive me for asking for Your mercy
at times when I did not show mercy to others.

Grant me faith that expects great things.
Give me insight to recognize Your answers.
Help me perceive my role in Your answers.

Never do I want to be a hypocrite again.
I want to do Your will.
I'm willing, Lord, to live for You.

Fill me with Your Holy Spirit.
Help me become all I can be.

"Therefore do not be anxious about tomorrow,
for tomorrow will be anxious for itself.
Let the day's own trouble be sufficient
for the day."

Matthew 6:34

"Have no anxiety about anything,
but in everything by prayer and supplication
with thanksgiving let your requests
be made known to God. And the peace of God,
which passes all understanding, will keep
your hearts and your minds in Christ Jesus."

Philippians 4:6,7

"Cast all your anxieties on Him,
for He cares about you."

1 Peter 5:7

"If God is for us, who is against us?
He who did not spare His own Son
but gave Him up for us all, will He not also
give us all things with Him?"

Romans 8:31,32

Don't Worry

The street bustled; trucks and cars roared by. But the two-year-old skipped along laughing excitedly. He was savoring the commotion. He didn't have any idea how he'd get across the traffic, but that didn't worry him. He was safe and secure clinging to his daddy's hand. All was well with his world.

Wouldn't it be great if we adults could face present dangers and the unknown future with such trust and confidence! Too often we act as if we are not sure that our Father is holding our hand, protecting and guiding us on our way!

As we go along in life, we store up all sorts of memories. When problems arise, we rehearse past perils — those we've experienced and those we've heard about from others. We try to anticipate every conceivable danger and disaster. That's supposed to prepare us. Instead it often just worries us.

If we burden our mind with troubles which may or may not happen, we weary and weaken ourselves. Some people lie awake at night picturing difficulties they may have tomorrow. Their lack of sleep may make them less able to cope with situations that actually do occur.

Jesus reminds us: "Do not be anxious about your life, what you shall eat. . . . Look at the birds . . . your heavenly Father feeds them." (Matthew 6:25,26)

We ask our Father for daily bread. He doesn't deliver it neatly wrapped to our doorstep. God doesn't do that for the birds either. They have to work for it. So do we. Our wise and loving Father doesn't do for us anything we can do for ourselves. If for some reason we cannot help ourselves, He will provide for us.

We plan and prepare for the future. But we should concentrate on the here and now. We can handle today. We can manage each tomorrow when it comes, with the help of God.

We need not torture ourselves worrying: Suppose my health fails? What if I lose my job? What will happen if . . .? Meditating on God's promises gets rid of such negative, discouraging thoughts.

We are apt to worry more if we just sit around dreading the unknown. Keeping busy — especially if we're busy serving others — helps replace worry.

We are to do everything we can do. What is beyond our control we are to leave to our loving heavenly Father.

Replace Worry with Faith

He should have been home long ago.
What could be wrong?

I hope he hasn't had car trouble.
Perhaps he's had an accident.
Could he be lying somewhere injured?
Has someone taken him to a hospital?
Why don't they phone to let me know?

Lord, help me erase these imaginings from my mind.
Why do I always assume the worst?
Is it because the news I hear and read
has filled my mind with unpleasant pictures?

Such thoughts do not strengthen me.
Nor do they help him in any way.

Lord, I must remind myself again and again:
I need fear no evil for You are with me.
You are also watching over those I love — near and far.
Your love is boundless.
You supply in time of need, protect in peril.
You give us strength in trouble, companionship in trials.
Please bring my loved one home safe.
Lord, I believe; help my unbelief.

Thank You, Lord. I hear his car in the driveway.
Help me not to snap:
"Where have you been? I've been worried sick!"
Help me let him know I'm thankful he is here.
Enable me to be understanding and
to give a good witness to my faith in You.

"Do not fear, only believe."

Mark 5:36

"The Lord is my light and my salvation;
whom shall I fear?
The Lord is the stronghold of my life;
of whom shall I be afraid?"

Psalm 27:1

"He has said,
'I will never fail you nor forsake you.'
Hence we can confidently say,
'The Lord is my helper,
I will not be afraid;
what can man do to me?'"

Hebrews 13:5,6

Face Your Fears

"I have a mortal fear of height," the woman confided after she had made a long plane trip. When asked how she had managed, she replied, "I knew I had to go; so I took an aisle seat and didn't look out the window." She had refused to let fear limit her pleasure and usefulness.

All of us are afraid at times. Only fools are never afraid.

Psychologists tell us we are born with two basic fears — fear of loud noises and fear of falling. Over the years we accumulate countless others. Some are good; others, bad.

Fear can range from fright and panic to prudence and foresight, awe and reverence.

Fear is the elemental alarm system God built into us. When we are faced with danger, fear triggers the production of adrenalin. This speeds heart action preparing us for fight or flight. When our fears cause us only to cower and cringe, the adrenalin meant to be a tonic becomes instead a poison. Chronic fear like a continuous false alarm wears out our body.

Fears can rob us of self-esteem. They inhibit us. We lose confidence, withdraw from life. We no longer believe we can cope with the problems and challenges that threaten us.

Jesus once asked His disciples, "Why are you afraid? Have you no faith?" Faith and fear are opposites. The more of one, the less of the other. Faith overcomes crippling fear.

One fear is necessary. The Bible commands us: fear the Lord! To fear the Lord is to revere and respect Him.

The more we respect and love the Lord, the more confidently we trust Him. The more we fear the Lord, the less we fear people and other experiences.

The most drastic and effective remedy for fear is direct action:

Ask God to help you overcome fear.
Trust He will.
Believe that with His help you can do anything
that has to be done.

Talk about your fears with others.
Be willing not only to share your qualms
but also to take advice.
Learn how others have coped with their fears.

Do the thing you fear.
Get started! If you can't take giant steps,
take baby steps.
If, for example, you're afraid to witness to
your faith, start with a gentle friend at the
first opportunity. Work up to unbelievers
and strangers.

If you're afraid to talk in front of a group,
force yourself into it. Don't begin by broadcasting
your fright. This may weaken your resolve and
ability to improve.

Be concerned for others.
In helping others you not only brighten their
lives, but you forget your own fear.
You are bravest when you act on behalf of those you
love or for a cause to which you are committed.

*   *   *   *

Face your fears courageously.
You will add excitement and zest to your life.

Fears Need Not Stop You

Lord,
help me to be afraid only
of the right things at the right times.

I am afraid
I may not be able to do all that is expected of me.
I may be criticized,
rejected, rebuffed.

Lord, help me remember
You've used cowards before.

Moses was afraid he couldn't handle his assignment.
Jonah turned and ran away from Your presence.
Gideon in fear acted under cover of darkness.
Peter was afraid of the sea and a servant girl.

In every case they finally came to the point
where they risked putting their lives into Your hands.
Though they were uncertain and afraid,
they did what You wanted them to do.
You used them to accomplish Your purposes.

Lord Jesus, You tell me I am the salt of the earth,
the light of the world.
You have more confidence in me
than I have in myself.

Granted, I am afraid.
What difference does that make!
Your confidence in me gives me confidence in myself.
I will do what You tell me to do.
I believe You'll go with me to gird and to guide.

"For I, the Lord your God,
hold your right hand;
it is I who say to you, 'Fear not,
I will help you.' "

Isaiah 41:13

"Be strong, and let your heart take courage,
all you who wait for the Lord!"

Psalm 31:24

"Be watchful, stand firm in your faith,
be courageous, be strong."

1 Corinthians 16:13

"The Lord is my strength and my shield. . . ."

Psalm 28:7

You Can Take It!

"I can't take it any more," the woman said when she asked for a transfer. She had been answering customer complaints for the power and light company. "Electric bills are now so high they hurt. When people call, some are angry, some abusive, others pathetic. There's nothing I can do. I just can't take it any more."

Many people can sympathize. They, too, live or work under great stress. Punch that clock. Pull that file. Pound that machine. Push that pencil. Turn that wheel. Lift that load. Hurry! Wait!

It's not only the major catastrophes that cause tension. Often it's a series of small matters.

When that woman said, "I can't take it any more," she really meant, "I've had enough. I'm not going to take it any more."

Sometimes people cannot leave their situation. They're trapped. Tension mounts. Dissatisfaction, frustration and anger grow. Troubles appear overwhelming. Life seems to be a hopeless race to nowhere.

Just saying, "I can't take it any more," develops a negative thought pattern. It lessens the probability of succeeding.

You can live a victorious life — despite all the potentially defeating factors that gang up against you. But it takes conscious effort.

Reach out to God.
Talk frankly with Him about your problem.
Don't waste your energy challenging His goodness.
Don't spend prayer time asking Him: why? why me?
God never promised to remove all the stress
from the lives of His faithful people.
Concentrate on the solution to your problem.
Tell God you can't take it without His help.
Ask Him for wisdom, patience, endurance, courage.

Expect God to answer.
"If we ask anything according to His will, He hears us. And if we know that He hears us — whatever we ask — we know that we have what we asked of Him." (1 John 5:14,15 NIV)

God doesn't do for you what you can do for yourself. You can't just whimper in a corner while He solves all your problems.

Begin to live in such a way that you're part of God's answer.

Little by little you'll experience victory over a problem that seemed tough, a situation that seemed impossible.

Each success, even a small one, builds up confidence.

You'll be encouraged to tackle the next phase of the problem.

Remind yourself repeatedly of this powerful truth:

"I can do all things in Him who strengthens me." (Philippians 4:13)

The apostle Paul wrote this. He was beaten, stoned, shipwrecked.

He suffered danger, hardship, sleepless nights, hunger, thirst, cold, separation from loved ones.

Yet he was sure God had a purpose for his life.

That drove him onward with certain conviction.

God has a purpose for your life, too.

He will enable you to fulfill it.

Accept help from others.

God often answers prayer through other people.

He may use the resources of a pastor, doctor, or lawyer.

He may guide you through the advice of a wise Christian friend.

Perhaps you need the encouragement of a hug or a listening ear.

Discern God's goodness in the help given by others.

Praise Him for it. Praise them for it, too.

Your thankful attitude makes it easier for others to help you.

Live with confidence.

Assure yourself:

> I am special.
> God loves me.
> God is with me.
> God is within me.
> I can do all things in Christ who strengthens me.
> God will help me! Yes, He will!
> I can take it! Yes, I can!

"The Lord disciplines him whom He loves."

Hebrews 12:6

*"So take a new grip with your tired hands,
stand firm on your shaky legs, and
mark out a straight, smooth path for your feet. . . ."*

Hebrews 12:12,13 TLB

*"And after you have suffered a little while,
the God of all grace, who has called you
to His eternal glory in Christ,
will Himself restore, establish,
and strengthen you."*

1 Peter 5:10

Keep On Going

Life at times is a succession of problems.
We may weaken under stress and pain —
be devastated by trauma or tragedy.

It's OK for us to cry.
That's why God gave us crying equipment.
Tears are a normal response. They give some relief.
Tears are a signal to others that we are hurting —
a quiet plea for sympathy, understanding or help.

But at some point we must stop crying
and talking about our problems.
Just feeling sorry for ourselves solves nothing.
After a while it turns others off.
We must begin to think coolly and objectively.
We have to help ourselves. We may have to seek help.
Perhaps we need advice, a helping hand, a lift,
or just a hug or an encouraging word.

We may not understand why life has taken the turn it has.
We wish our problems were not so many or so difficult.
God has allowed life to be the way it is.
He can use problems to develop our character.
Sometimes important accomplishments grow out of tragedy.

God has not promised skies always blue.
There will be clouds, rain, thunder — even tornadoes.
But we are not alone.
Through every experience, through every change
God is with us. He will give us strength.

When finally we are graduated from this vale of tears,
we will have no problems.
In heaven there is only perfect joy and peace.
Meanwhile God has some purpose for our lives.
He really needs us and is depending on us.
Though we falter and fall, we have to get up and keep on going.

Forgive Yourself

"If only I had . . ."
"I wish I had never . . ."
Such torturing thoughts accomplish nothing.
It's often hard to forgive ourselves
for stupid mistakes, careless acts, wrong decisions.
But regrets cannot undo the past.
They only weigh us down and lower our self-esteem.

God forgives our sins and mistakes.
The blood of Jesus cleanses us from all sin.
We confess our sins and desire not to commit them again.
Since God offers complete forgiveness,
we should accept it and forgive ourselves.

God does not always remove the consequences.
We may have to live with memories of
wasted opportunities, wasted assets, wasted years.
Sometimes we can make amends,
but reparation is not always possible.

Still we can be optimistic.
God isn't finished with us yet!
We're still under construction.
We know we have faults. It is a struggle to improve.
No one has it all together.
How patient we ought to be with fellow strugglers!

We need to learn to pick ourselves up,
dust ourselves off and start all over again.

We can learn from past experiences
and determine for the future:
"Never again will I. . . ."
"With God's help the next time I will. . . ."

Take Heart

Lord,
I've failed!
Failure is hard to bear.
It hurts my ego, weakens my will, drains my energy.

Help me believe that this failure
doesn't mean I'm a failure.

Keep me from being envious
lest I resent those who succeed.

What do You want me to learn from my failure?
What mistakes should I avoid?
Help me become wiser.
Give me strength to correct my faults
and overcome my weaknesses.

Where I can never be different,
teach me acceptance.
Where You and I together can change me,
show me my part.

Lord,
I may fail — once, twice, many times.
Yet You never say, "Sorry, you've had your chance."
Thank You, Lord, for new beginnings.

"Bless the Lord, O my soul,
and forget not all His benefits . . .
who satisfies you with good
as long as you live. . . ."

Psalm 103:2,5

"They who wait for the Lord
shall renew their strength,
they shall mount up with wings like eagles,
they shall run and not be weary,
they shall walk and not faint."

Isaiah 40:31

"As your days,
so shall your strength be."

Deuteronomy 33:25

Admit Your Age

Birthdays are good for me.
The more I have, the longer I'll live.

Some people have stopped having birthdays.
Their bodies lie in cold and silent spots —
felled by illness, mishap or worn-out parts.

Why should I who still have life and breath
apologize for having birthdays!
Why should I be embarrassed to admit my age!
No one asked me what year I wanted to be born.
Since I began at an earlier date than others, I'm older than they.
There's no need to be ashamed because I've been around longer.
Nor have I a right to brag that I arrived later than some.
They had no choice either.

I'm not afraid of getting old, though I do not look forward to
fading beauty, wrinkling skin, sagging frame, failing health,
diminishing strength, dimming eyesight, forgetful mind.

It's my Christian duty to make the most of what I am and have.
I ought to look my best, think my best, act my best —
for my own sake and for the sake of those I may be able to help.
Good nutrition and health habits and a positive outlook
help keep my body and mind in sound condition.
But I cannot prevent time from rolling on
or this tent of flesh from getting out of repair.
Yet the spirit that lives in it need not shrivel and dry up.

I must open my mind to new ideas, new ways of doing things.
I need to keep growing, smiling and
believing God has a purpose for my life.
He still can do something in me and through me.

So many years and good things of life are now behind me.
I enjoy looking back at them in fond recollection.
But God put eyes in the front of my head.
He must want me to look forward to what is yet to be.

I'm still having birthdays! Praise the Lord!

Are You Chasing Rainbows?

Somewhere over the rainbow . . .
things must be better than they are here.

Some people think they would be happy
if only they had waited,
if only they had done this or that,
if only a spouse or child would shape up.

They are convinced contentment would be theirs
if only they had a different job,
if only they could make more money,
if only they lived elsewhere.

Some only dream of the future.
"One of these days things will be better."
"One of these days my ship will come in."
"One of these days I might . . ."

They are wrong.

This life is to be lived and enjoyed here and now.
We have a one-time-only opportunity to be.
Each of us has only one chance.
We do not know how long our turn will last.

"This is the day which the Lord has made;
let us rejoice and be glad in it." (Psalm 118:24)

Every day we must do the best we can to serve the Lord
where we are
with what we have
and what we are.

Life is a one-way street.
If there is any good we can do,
let's not defer or neglect it.
We'll never pass this way again.

Thank God for Today

Thank You, Lord,
for the gift of today.
Keep me mindful that in a higher sense
today is not a gift. Time is Yours.
You're only letting me use it.

Many demands will be made of me.
Help me set the proper priorities,
to distinguish between the important and the trivial.
Guide me to use my day wisely and efficiently.

I need 8 hours to sleep, 8 hours to do my work,
and 4 hours for other essentials of living.
That leaves me 240 valuable minutes.
What should I do with these little snatches of time
sandwiched in throughout the day?

I need time to be with You — to refresh my spirit —
to read and meditate upon Your Word.

I need time to relax,
to recreate my mind, to exercise my body.
All work and no play can make me dull.
All play makes me selfish and useless.

Lord, You want me to love my neighbor as myself.
Make me aware of opportunities to serve.
I'll budget my time so I have time for others.
Perhaps it will be only a phone call or a brief note.
But I'll find time today to do something for somebody else.

When my time runs out, I'll no doubt
have some things of value to pass on to others.
But I will have no time to bequeath.
Remind me to spend time with those I love
while there is still time.

Use Time Wisely

Some days we think we have all the time in the world.
We have time on our hands.
We're tempted to kill time — as if it were an enemy!

Other days we try to save time —
though it cannot be stored for future use.
We cannot make up for lost time.
Nor can we really live on borrowed time.
We complain we do not have enough time —
or that we have no time.
Only the dead have no time.

Occasionally time seems to stand still or just crawl.
But time marches on.
Often we discover time flies.
We say time goes by.
But, no! Time stays. It is we who come and go.

The earth keeps spinning at the same rate.
No one has more than 24 hours each day.
The relative speed of time depends on us —
whether we're young or old, bored or busy,
having an awful time or a wonderful time.

We try to race against time.
That makes us nervous and uneasy.
We wish time away.
Watching the clock, we wish it were time to go.
In other cases, we'd like to turn back the clock
and have another chance to relive the time.

Time is a blessing we must not take for granted.
It is one of God's great gifts.
Like grace, time is given, not earned.
It is a sacred trust for which we must some day give accounting.
Time is opportunity. We use it or lose it.
Time is life. It is precious.
Time is the most valuable thing we can spend!

Do It Now

"Never put off till tomorrow what can be done today." We've heard that since childhood. But too often we make exceptions to that old rule.

Of course, some actions must be postponed for good reason. Many actions, however, are put off for poor reasons. Our excuses?

Maybe we feel too tired. As a matter of fact, we feel less tired on busy, well-planned days. Boring, aimless days make us more tired and listless.

Perhaps we don't feel just right. Yet most of the world's work is done by people who don't feel very good at the time.

We may think we don't have time. Most of us need more character, not more time. If we set goals and program ourselves, we get the necessary things done. We also have time to help others and to do things we like to do.

Once in a while we just can't make up our minds. So we delay decisions. We wait and wait. We should wait on the Lord; trust Him to guide us; be alert to His direction through people and circumstances; then forge ahead.

If we are creative, we are often perfectionists. We want to do something different, special, just right. So we put it off hoping for a golden moment. The best motivation for inspiration is pressure.

Sometimes we pass up today's opportunities by telling ourselves things will improve tomorrow. Once missed, many opportunities never return.

Procrastination is an enemy. It is the thief of time. It causes anxiety, stress, frustration. We weary ourselves thinking about what ought to be done. We condemn ourselves for not doing it.

Life is now! Only today is ours. Yesterday has slipped through our fingers. Tomorrow lives only in our imagination.

Life is short. We must not let it get away from us by default.
What have you been putting off?
Do it now.
You'll feel better about yourself.

Be All You Can Be

Lord Jesus,
I praise You for being my Savior.
You lived a perfect life on my behalf.
Thank You for dying in my place,
paying in full the penalty of my sin.
Because of You I'm saved from its eternal consequences.
Now I'm free!

But I'm not free to be me!
You've purchased and won me.
I'm Yours.
I'm free — to serve You!
Only when I want to do what You want me to do
am I really free!

I want to please You, but it's hard to put aside
my own will, my pride, my fears.

I want to do Your will, but often I try to juggle it with mine.
My mind and heart want to go their own way.
I seem to hope that when all Your demands are met,
I can get on with my own desires and dreams.

I see tasks that should be done,
needs that are crying to be met.
Forgive me for often just sitting around
waiting for You to take care of these problems.
You want me to be Your tongue, Your hands, Your feet.

At times it takes something on our part
for You to do what You promise.
You once told a man, "Put out your hand." You healed it.
To another You said, "Go wash in the pool."
You restored his sight.
To me You say, "Knock, and it will be opened to you."
"Give, and it will be given to you."
"Go . . . and lo, I am with you."

You don't do for me what I can do myself.
What a wise and loving Lord You are!

Without me there are some things You will not do.
Without You there is nothing I can do.

Lord, I want to be like You.
Teach me; train me; mold me; use me.

Take me. I'm Yours.

DO ALL YOU CAN DO

God made you.
You are special.
He called you to be His child.

God loves you.
Love yourself.
Be all you can be.

You are God's gift to the world.
Do all you can do
to make it a better place.

God Calls You

You love me, Lord?
That truth is impossible to fathom.

Sometimes I'm happy with myself.
But many, many times
I'm disappointed, discouraged, disgusted.

How could You love me?
You are perfect!
How can You go on loving
and forgiving?

Why did You lay down Your life for me?
Grace! Undeserved love!
But why me?
Me of all people!

Dear Jesus,
You didn't call me
just to sit and try to comprehend the mind of God.
You call me to follow You,
to go, to be a witness,
to be salt, light.

You expect me not to understand Your love,
but to believe it,
to share it with others.

You promise to be with me always,
to empower me with Your Spirit.
Mold me, Lord, into an instrument of Your love.

You love me, Lord!
That truth is impossible to fathom.
But it warms my heart! It lights up my life!

Be Willing to Serve

Heavenly Father,
thank You for loving me,
for accepting me in Christ just as I am.

Nobody else knows me as well as You do.
I put up a pretty good front,
but You see right through my mask.

Others often think I'm somebody I'm really not.
At times I try to become the me
that I think they expect me to be.
Instead I should become the me
You want me to be.
You want me to be like Jesus.

Father,
I've got to stop looking in the mirror
and look out the window instead.

Help me remember You put me where I am
at this stage of my life for some good reason.
There must be something
which only I can do for You.
If I don't do it, perhaps it will never be done.

Help me discern what You want me to be doing,
to recognize anyone You want me to help today.

I'm willing to serve, Father.
Use me in Your service.

Let God Use You

I gave my neighbor a ride today. It was only a few minutes out of my way. When I dropped her off at her house, she thanked me and added, "God sent you." Her bag of groceries was heavier than she had expected, and she had murmured, "O Lord, how will I ever make it home!"

It had seemed so casual an incident to me. I just happened to need a few things from the store. I just happened to have the car. Both of us just happened to be checking out at the same time.

Did God know her problem even before she did? Did He arrange my schedule so that I would be at the right place at the right time?

This morning I had prayed my day would be worthwhile in God's sight. This incident must have been part of God's plan. He used me to answer my neighbor's prayer.

I didn't hear any special voice. No unusual prodding moved me. And yet . . . there was a phone call just as I was ready to leave for the store. I was annoyed. It seemed a poor time to listen for ten minutes to the problems of a friend. Was that also part of His plan? Was that delay meant to put me on schedule to meet my neighbor at the moment of her need?

The Lord watches over the lives of all His children. How our lives must intertwine! How the prayers of one must affect the rest!

O Lord, thank You for using me today to share Jesus' love — as a listening post for my friend and a lift for my neighbor. Those were small favors to ask of me, those few moments of my time.

Forgive me for not offering myself in Your service every day. What opportunities I must have missed! Use me, Lord!

Ephesians 2:10   For we are God's workmanship, created in Christ Jesus to do good works, which God prepared in advance for us to do.

Your Role Is Important

Lord Jesus,
I am only a tiny cog
in a world of wheels!

The chores I have to do today
will not take a great amount of skill.
They require patience, endurance.

Lord, help me remember:
You love me. I am special.
I'm precious in Your sight.

There is a purpose for my life.
You put me where I am
because You have things for me to do.
You depend on me to serve my neighbors.

What I do for the least of them
I am doing for You.
I depend on You to cheer me on.

Dear Savior, lubricate me with the oil
of Your forgiving love
so the world runs more smoothly because of me.

I am an important cog
in a world of wheels.

"A new commandment I give to you,
that you love one another;
even as I have loved you,
that you also love one another.
By this all men will know that
you are My disciples,
if you have love for one another."

John 13:34, 35

"We love, because He first loved us . . .
he who does not love his brother
whom he has seen, cannot love God
whom he has not seen.
And this commandment we have from Him,
that he who loves God should love
his brother also."

1 John 4:19–21

"Love your enemies,
do good to those who hate you ."

Luke 6:27

Love All God's Children

"Stick together! Help each other!"
That's advice a wise and loving father gave his children.
What an advantage they have —
each surrounded by a ready-made support group!

This gives us a small glimpse of
God's grand design for the whole human family —
now more than four billion in the world.
Our heavenly Father wants us to help one another.
What wholeness we would know if we obeyed His command:
"Love your neighbor as yourself."

WHAT is this thing called love?
God does not mean that we express passion for our neighbor.
Nor does He mean that we only have sympathy for others.
It's not enough to feel sorry for those with problems.
Love is an imperative verb!
Love moved God to give His Son.
Loving our neighbor requires us to do something —
to spend time, energy or material goods.

WHO is our neighbor?
Anyone to whom we can be a neighbor.
With present-day communication and transportation
our neighbor can be someone far beyond the horizon —
        or next door.
Some people who most need our love are unlovely.
Others whom we try to love prove to be unloving.

HOW can we love even those who turn us off?
It's not always easy to love our neighbor!
In fact it's downright impossible
without God's motivation and strength.
"We love, because He first loved us." (1 John 4:19)
Our heavenly Father loves us though we are
undeserving, uncooperative, ungrateful.
He loves without expectation of reward or repayment.
As He loves us, we are to love others.

118

WHY do we love our neighbor?
Because "God's love has been poured into our hearts."
(Romans 5:5)
God wants us to express His love —
to love Him with all our heart,
with all our soul, and with all our mind
and to love our neighbor as ourselves.
If we really love our heavenly Father, we love His other children.
Only in God's love do we find our purpose in life.
Only in God's love do we find power to fulfill it.

*"Since we have the same spirit of faith
as he had who wrote,
'I believed, and so I spoke,'
we too believe, and so we speak."*

2 Corinthians 4:13

*"My mouth will tell of Thy righteous acts,
of Thy deeds of salvation all the day . . . ."*

Psalm 71:15

*"Go home to your friends, and
tell them how much the Lord has done for you,
and how He has had mercy on you."*

Mark 5:19

*"You are a chosen race, a royal priesthood,
a holy nation, God's own people,
that you may declare the wonderful deeds of
Him who called you out of darkness
into His marvelous light."*

1 Peter 2:9

*"Be ready at all times to answer anyone
who asks you to explain the hope you have in you,
but do it with gentleness and respect."*

1 Peter 3:15, 16 GNB

Talk About Jesus

Dear Lord Jesus,
thank You for the confidence You have in me.
When You say, "You shall be My witness,"
You give me a noble task.

Thank You for leaving the Father's home on high
and coming to earth to be my Savior.
You taught, healed, raised the dead,
calmed the storm, fed multitudes, washed feet!
Yet You were despised and rejected.
You allowed men to torture and kill You.
But You rose victorious from the grave
to complete the plan of salvation made before time began.

Because You died for me, I have eternal life!
I am free from the eternal punishment for my sins.
Our Father laid on You the sins of us all —
all the sins of all the people of all the world!

Many don't know it yet!
They need to hear the Good News.
You don't send angels to broadcast it.
You use ordinary people like me.

Forgive me, Lord, for often being too busy
with my own affairs to tell others about You.

Forgive me for not caring about multitudes who
will spend eternity without hope unless they trust You.

Forgive me for times when I invited people to my church
but failed to talk to them about You.
The church doesn't save. You do.

Forgive me for being too timid to speak of Your
day-by-day care, Your answers to my prayers.

Forgive me for being too afraid of ridicule
to speak of my faith in You.
You suffered torture and death for me!

Forgive me for assuming the way I live
is enough to communicate my faith.
How arrogant that is!
My life is not so transparent
that Your love shines through!
I need to speak in clear-cut words the Good News
that adds joy, peace and love to life!

Forgive me for failing to speak about my faith
because I wasn't really sure what I believed —
and had haunting self-doubts.

Stir me, Lord, to equip myself to be a better witness.
I want to know You better, Your Word, Your will for my life.
I want to be ever learning, ever growing,
ever becoming more like You.

Open my eyes to recognize the opportunities
You give me today to tell someone about You.

Open my mouth to speak words of comfort and hope.

I've often come to You for solace.
Now I offer to be Your messenger.

Use me, Lord Jesus, as an instrument
to bring Your love to others,
to bring others to You.

Demonstrate God's Love

"The Word
became flesh
and dwelt among us." *(John 1:14)*

God
still wraps
the Good News in human flesh.
I take
His message
out into the world.

What
do people
learn about the love of God
when
they see me
where I live and work and shop?

Do
they see Jesus?
Or do I blot out that view
by
the things
I think and say and do?

Lord,
help me
to demonstrate Your love,
so
others know
You live in me and I in You.

Receive Graciously

"Mmmm! This cake is delicious," he said.
I shrugged. "It's only a package cake."

"I like your dress."
It was a compliment.
I replied, "It's something I've had for years."

"Your hair looks nice."
My response:
"It's much too long. I'm having it cut tomorrow."

"You did so well today. Congratulations!"
"I should have done much better. . . ."

O Lord!
I meant to be humble.
Yet all I did was humiliate others.

In effect I said to those who paid me a compliment:
"You are a poor judge of quality and style."
I meant to put myself down.
I put them down instead.

Forgive me, Lord Jesus,
for putting anybody down — others or me.

Help me remember to
return kindness with kindness:
"I'm glad you like it."
"How nice of you to say that."
"How kind you are to notice."
"I thank you, and I thank God."

Lord, help me be a gracious receiver.

Say "Thank You"

Many doors are opened with two magic keys.
One of them is "thank you"; the other one is "please."

Most parents teach their little children to use
these tokens of good manners and good sense.
If a two-year-old forgets to respond with "Thank you,"
the parent prods, "What do you say?"

Sometimes grown-ups need such prodding.
We are apt to take the service of others for granted —
especially when we didn't have to coax them to perform.

Nobody likes to be overlooked or unappreciated.

Have you ever held a door open for someone
who passed by without even a nod of acknowledgement?
You'd like to ask, "What do you say?"

When we fail to express our gratitude to those
in the home, at work, in the community or congregation,
we diminish them.
We may lessen their desire to do good in the future.

When we love our neighbors, we obey the Lord.
We react to His immense love for us.
Whether or not they express gratitude
should not hinder us from pleasing Him.

Yet a "thank you" does gladden the heart.
It encourages us to be helpful and kind.

"Let us consider how to stir up one another
to love and good works." (Hebrews 10:24)

A sincere "thank you" helps to stir.

"A word in season, how good it is!"

Proverbs 15:23

*"Pleasant words are like a honeycomb,
sweetness to the soul and health to the body."*

Proverbs 16:24

*"If there is any excellence,
if there is anything worthy of praise,
think about these things."*

Philippians 4:8

Have a Word of Praise

The tollgate at the bridge was a busy place that morning. But as the collector handed change to the driver, he added, "That's a good-looking suit!" What a surprise! Toll collectors usually say only, "Thank you." Did he say something pleasant to every driver that day? Who knows! But this driver went off smiling, feeling good about herself, more cheerful the rest of the day. A little compliment can go a long way!

It makes us vulnerable when we say a kind word to others. They may not accept our remark in the way we expect. Some people don't know how to receive a compliment graciously. That's their problem! We should not be hindered by their failure.

When we are too timid or reluctant to compliment others, they are diminished. We are, too. If we bless others with an encouraging word, we, too, are blessed.

Building up people is not flattery. It is honestly encouraging the talents and attractive traits we observe in others. This requires looking for the loveliness in people. In the process we become more lovely.

Sociologists tell us we become what we think other people think we are. We expand or shrink to fit the image we believe others have of us.

Extravagant praise may swell a person's head. Lack of praise may shrivel the heart.

An encouraging word is not indiscriminate applause: "You're the best secretary in the whole world." It is more realistic and helpful to say, "I admire your pleasant manner on the phone. You did a good job with these letters. You handled that situation very well." Honest praise nourishes the good qualities in people.

When the bank teller is cheerful, we might tell her we appreciate it. If the checker at the store is capable, we can say a word of praise. As we observe well-behaved children, we can tell them how nicely they act. Their parents also will be cheered by such a comment.

For all of us life is a struggle. Often it is a hard, lonely battle. Jesus strengthens us that we may encourage one another, build each other up. When we say something kind, we speak God's word of hope. We help others become what they are capable of being.

Lend an Ear

The four-year-old hurried down the aisle in the supermarket. Eagerly he went from one customer to another with the exciting news: "You know what I just saw? A big bug!" The reaction of the shoppers ranged from stony silence to a disgusted, "Ugh!"

All of us at times need someone who will listen. We want to be given attention, to feel significant. We'd like to cry out, "Friends, Romans, countrymen, lend me your ears," as Mark Antony did when he wanted an audience.

When we're bubbling over with good news, our joy is heightened by sharing it. If we're crushed by disappointment or sorrow, it helps to verbalize our feelings. When a problem has downed us, we may wish to discuss it with someone who'll try to understand.

We look for an ear to borrow. Too few offer one to lend.

When we are listened to, we unfold and expand. Ideas come to life and grow within us. A good listener builds up our self-esteem.

We need to listen to what another wants to tell us and not pry information the teller may not be ready to share. Questions may stimulate the speaker to think more clearly. "Is this what you mean? what you're really trying to say?"

Effective listening communicates interest in the speaker. We strive to listen to others the way we want God to listen to us who love Jesus — with full attention.

Loving our neighbor sometimes requires lending a hand. Often we must be willing to lend an ear.

Speak an Encouraging Word

When people ask us to lend them our ears,
sometimes we offer instead a piece of our mind.

If a person tells you in confidence something stupid he has done,
be slow to criticize.
Don't say, "Whatever made you do such a thing?" or
"Well, I warned you . . . . You should have. . . ."
He needs someone to hear the confession.
Don't turn him off.
Help him figure out what can be done about the situation.

When someone tells you of an evil thing he's done,
try not to act shocked. Don't be quick to judge.
Try to understand what made him act as he did.
God wants to love him through you.
Gently remind him: "God forgives for Jesus' sake. So do I.
Tomorrow is a new chance to begin again."

Boost the confidence of the person
who comes to you to talk about her troubles.
Express belief in her ability to cope and eventually conquer.
Talking about her problem relieves some tensions,
helps crystallize her convictions.
Help her to sort out the facts.
Don't make decisions for her:
"You ought to . . . . If he were my husband, I'd. . . ."

It's hard to listen to some people.
They wallow in self-pity, constantly harping on their woes.
Do them a favor by listening for a while, and
then change the subject.
Say, "When I have troubles, I find it helpful to
stress the positive.
The Bible tells us, 'Give thanks in all circumstances.'
(1 Thessalonians 5:18) There must be some things for which you
can be thankful. Name a few and concentrate on them."

As opportunity arises, speak a word of encouragement.
Tell how God has answered your prayers.
Explain how your faith helped you through crises.
Witness to your confidence in God's love,
"What He has done for others, He will do for you."

Be Available

"It's been so good talking to you," she said.

O Lord, she tires my ears!
For half an hour she chattered on.
She lives alone and has nothing else to do.
Here I am, pulled this way and that by demands upon my time!

She wanted to talk about her heartaches.
Lord, I share those secrets only with You.
Help me not reveal facts told in confidence.
When she shared her problem with me,
she gave me a sacred trust not to be taken lightly.

Help me to love her as You do, Jesus,
without attempting to force on her
what I believe is the right thing to do.

I do not have a solution for her problem.
But, Lord, I know You do.
I bring her concerns to You and put them in Your hands.
Make Your will clear to her
and my responsibility clear to me.
Hold her firmly in the palm of Your hand.
Help her be more aware of Your loving presence,
more assured of Your almighty power.

Keep me from trying to impress her with my
holiness, intelligence, success, happiness.
Make me kind, tenderhearted, patient.

Lord, forgive my pride which resents
interruption of my schedule.
She needs to talk.
Help me to listen.

Forgive Others

"Father, forgive us as we have forgiven others."
That's what Jesus teaches us to pray.

It's hard to forgive someone who has done great injury to us.
It may be harder to forgive those who continually irritate us,
eroding our self-respect, destroying our happiness.
It's not easy to forgive even petty annoyances of daily life.

It wasn't easy for God to forgive either!
In fact, it was the hardest thing He did.
God's Son suffered hell for our sins.

"If we confess our sins, He is faithful and just,
and will forgive our sins. . . ." (1 John 1:9)
God forgives for Jesus' sake.
He no longer holds our sins against us.
They are forgiven forever.

When our hearts have been warmed by God's amazing,
forgiving love, we forgive others.

To forgive does not mean we can always forget.
The memory of a certain wrong may be so deep and
so painful we can not erase it from our mind.
To forgive does not require us to resume the same relation
we once had with the person we forgive.

To forgive means we do not hold grudges.
We do not seek revenge. The Lord says He will repay.
We do not humiliate or hurt those who hurt us.
We do not dig up and dwell on past wrongs.

To refuse to forgive others cuts us off from God.
It keeps us from proper worship and fellowship with God.
It prevents His power from entering our lives.

Nothing is more Godlike than to forgive.
Nothing is more necessary.

Pray for a Forgiving Heart

Gracious God,
through Jesus You forgive me over and over again!
You tell me to forgive others that way, too,
to pray for those who abuse me,
to do good to those who do evil to me.

Help!
I don't really want to do things Your way.
It's too tough! It doesn't seem fair!

Forgive me, Lord,
for my failures to obey You, my failures to love others.

I need to hear You say to me,
"Well, you blew it again. Confess it!
Accept My forgiveness. Now, give it another try."
Thanks for loving me, forgiving me.
I appreciate another chance.

That's what I should be doing for others, isn't it?

Lord, help me treat others the way You treat me.
I want to be like You,
forgiving others from my heart.
I can't do it on my own!
I need Your strength,
the encouragement of Your Spirit within me.

Use me in the beautiful work of
sharing Your forgiving love in this world.

Weep with Those Who Weep

When Jesus saw Mary weeping after her brother, Lazarus, died, Jesus also wept. He had compassion on the widow of Nain as she wept over the death of her son. Jesus' pity moved Him to do something.

Those who weep over the death of a loved one — or the death of a marriage — need compassion and also help. What can you do to let them know you care?

A visit at the time of loss is appreciated.
Probably even more important than attendance at the funeral is a visit long after the funeral is over.
That's when loneliness sets in.

In a divorce there is no funeral, no outpouring of love and sympathy. Yet the trauma is just as real.

Flowers add some cheer at the funeral,
but too many cannot possibly be appreciated. It is usually of more consolation to know that money has been given to the church or a favorite charity in memory of the deceased.

A small bouquet coming as a surprise in the lonesome weeks and months that follow brightens a sad heart.

A note may be valued more than a printed card.
In a few sentences tell of your concern.
Say something nice about the deceased — a pleasant memory, an experience you've shared.

It doesn't matter when you send the note.
Even a few months after the loss is all right.
The grieving process takes a long, long time.
Pray for the sorrowing. Ask God to strengthen and guide.
Tell them you pray for them.
Witness to your faith in Jesus who is
the Resurrection and the Life.

A phone call just to talk is helpful.
  Time is long for one who grieves.
  If you don't know what to say, let the mourner talk.

Listen to the grieving. Don't judge.
  Let them ramble and repeat.
  It helps them to talk about the details.

Advise the grieving
  not to be too hasty to move or make other drastic decisions,
  not to make a major change, if possible, for at least a year.

Invite the mourner for a meal.
  Learning to eat alone may be a hard adjustment.

Include the newly-singled in family events and affairs
  usually attended by couples.

Give a helping hand when you can.
  Don't say, "Let me know if I can do anything."
  The grieving may be too distressed or too proud to ask.
  Make a concrete offer: "What can I get for you at the store?"
  "I'll pick you up and take you to the meeting."
  "I'm bringing the cake. Put on the coffeepot."
  "I'll babysit next Monday."

Comfort also those with a strong faith.
  The promise of life with Jesus for a departed loved one
  does not eliminate the grief of the living.

  A Christian friend who is divorced needs sympathy
  and support — not condemnation or ostracism.

Be patient! Mourning often lasts for years.
  A death or divorce is like the amputation of a limb.
  One adjusts, but life is not the same.
  It never stops hurting; it only gets less painful.
  When we weep with those who weep,
  we help relieve their pain.

Follow Jesus

Only
once
did God
come to earth in the form of a man.

Did
He
dazzle us
with heavenly pomp and splendor?

No!
Christ
humbled Himself
and took the form of a servant!

Jesus
taught
us to love.
He went about doing good.

Lord,
forgive
me for often
just going about my own business.

Lord,
please
strengthen me
to take up my cross and follow You.

Smile

Draw a circle for a preschooler and say,
"Make a happy face."
Without hesitation the child will draw an upturned line.
Turn that curve upside down; now the face is sad or grumpy.
How much you can tell about a person
by the expression on the face!

It takes twenty-six muscles to frown
but only five muscles to smile.
Down with frowns. Be kind to your face. Smile!

A smile affects both the sender and the receiver.
It says, "I'm glad to see you. I wish you well."
We smile at others when they please us
and because we ourselves need to be smiled at.
We act as mirrors for one another.

A smile doesn't necessarily mean you feel good
or that all's well with your world.
A smile may mean that even though you're hurting,
you're thinking positively. Your life is under God's control.
He is in charge, and you have faith in Him.

A smile is especially important at church.
It says you're glad to be in God's house,
happy to be singing His praises and hearing His Word.

The grand Designer of heaven and earth made you.
He loves you. His precious Son died for you.
God laid all your sins on Jesus. You are free.
You can be rid of guilt, resentment and worry.
Your face can reflect God's goodness
so others see how great it is to know the living Lord.
If you have the joy of Jesus in your heart,
please notify your face.
For heaven's sake smile!

Pray for Others

Lord,
I do not understand
why certain things don't happen unless I pray.
My neighbors' needs are known to You before I speak.
You do not have to look to me for information or instruction.

Yet You encourage me to bring their wants before Your throne.
You say, "Pray for one another." (James 5:16)
It strengthens me to know others are praying for me.
My prayers help them.
We're linked together because we are Your children in Christ.

Forgive me for times I rush around too busy to pray
though there are so many moments I waste.
When I wait for appointments or in line at the store,
I could talk with You about the problems of friends.

While I do chores that need little thought,
I can turn my mind to You and the needs of others.
As I make the beds, I can pray for someone who is sick.
While my hands are busy dusting, I can pray
for someone who doesn't know Your love.
When I'm preparing food or cleaning up after a meal,
I might pray for the hungry of the world.

You are merciful and mighty. You can do all things.
Yet sometimes You wait for some action on my part.
Often You use an ordinary person like me
to accomplish Your purpose.

Lord, I'm willing to do all I can do.

Do Something for Someone

Sometimes I wonder,
"Why doesn't somebody do something?"

O Lord, help me realize
I might be that somebody.

When I suffer compassion fatigue,
sharpen my sensitivity to the needs of others.
Make me more conscious of Your concern for me in Jesus
that I may reflect it to others.

Wherever I am,
whatever shape I'm in,
however limited my opportunity,
may I never underestimate
my ability
to make the world
a little better
for someone else.

I cannot do everything,
but I can do something.
With Your help, Lord,
what I can do
I will do.

God Will Reward You

Doing unto others
can do wonderful things for you!

"Love your neighbor as yourself"
is not a law that blesses just your neighbor.
You, too, are blessed when you keep it.

When you're a helper, your self-image improves.
Life becomes more meaningful.
You feel you are worthwhile. You have a purpose.
This will have a positive effect upon your health!

Being active in volunteer work keeps you young in spirit.
Caring for others makes you less lonely.
Giving of yourself is an antidote to stress.

"It is more blessed to give than to receive." *(Acts 20:35)*
But you must give from the goodness of your heart.
If you're giving only to get something in return,
you'll be disappointed.

Sometimes your kindness will go unnoticed, but
"Your Father who sees in secret will reward you." *(Matthew 6:4)*

"Arise and be doing!
The Lord be with you!"
1 Chronicles 22:16